Essential Camera Skills

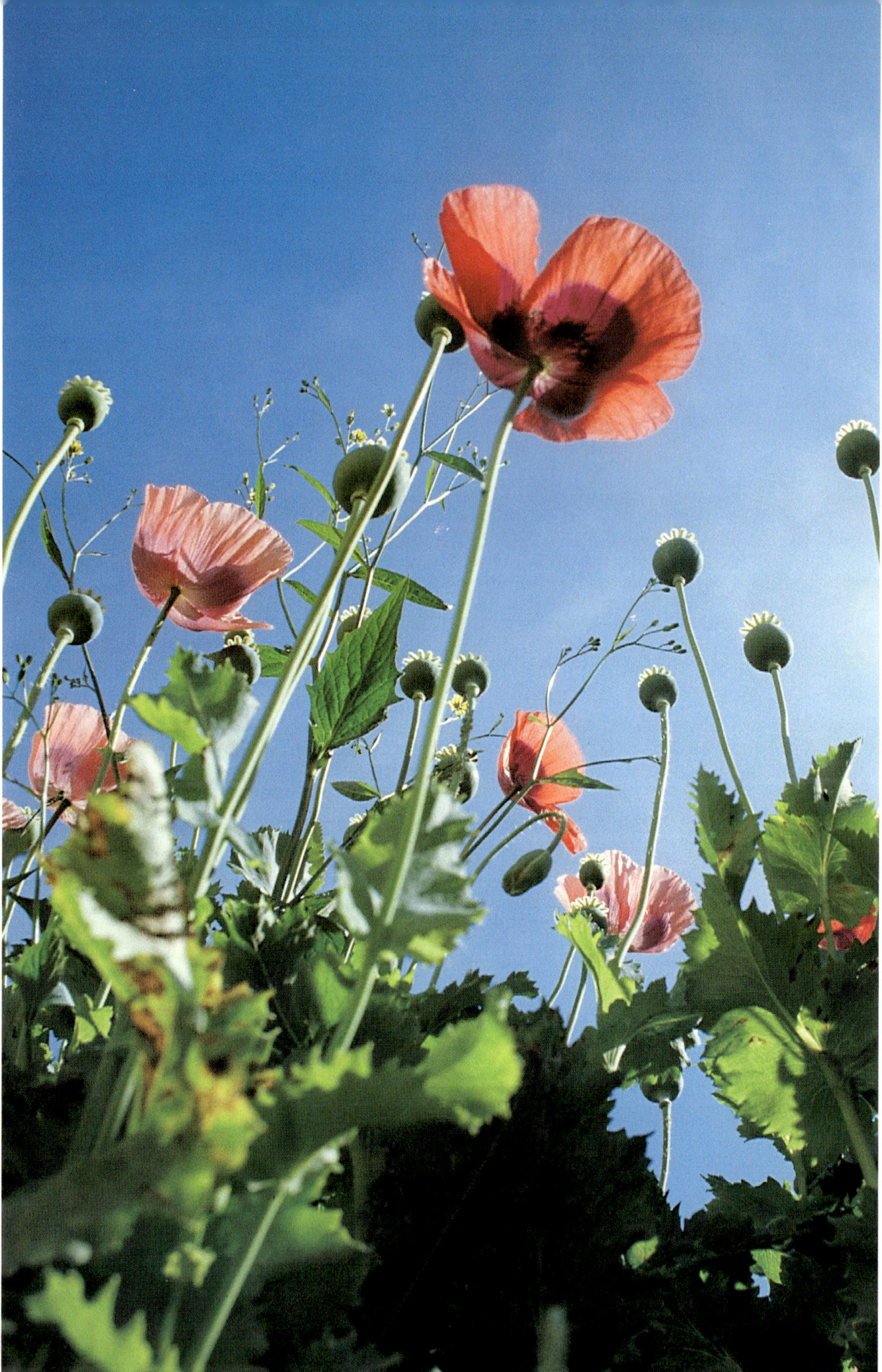

Essential Camera Skills

THE COMPLETE INTRODUCTORY GUIDE TO SLR PHOTOGRAPHY

Joël Lacey

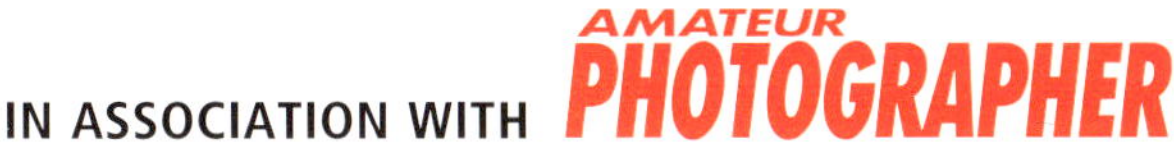

HAMLYN

Essential Camera Skills

First published in 1995 by Hamlyn,
an imprint of Reed Consumer Books Limited
Michelin House
81 Fulham Road
London SW3 6RB
and Auckland, Melbourne, Singapore and Toronto

Editor Kirsty Seymour-Ure
Designer Marc Riley
Production Controller Juliette Butler
Indexer Ann Barrett

Executive Editor Sarah Polden
Executive Art Editor Vivienne Brar
Art Director Jacqui Small

Typeset in Linotype Garamond and TradeGothic
Colour reproduction by Dot Gradations, Essex, England
Printed in Hong Kong

A CIP catalogue record for this book is available from the British Library.

ISBN 0 600 58627 8

Contents

The Camera

Taking photographs is easy. Kodak's first advertising slogan for a camera was 'You press the button, we do the rest'. But taking *good* photographs needs a little more thought, a knowledge of how a camera works, and a camera you can control.

All cameras are based around four components: a viewfinder, a lens, a shutter, and a mechanism that advances the film and keeps it flat. A single lens reflex (SLR) camera uses the same lens for viewing the image and for exposing the film. The fundamental advantage of this is that what you see through the viewfinder is what you get on the film.

The first SLR was designed in 1935, but it was not until 1957, with the Japanese Asahiflex (now known as Pentax), that the camera as we know it today emerged. In the early 1960s Nikon pioneered the motor drive (allowing several shots per second), and the SLR came into its own – notably during the Vietnam War – as the preferred choice of professional photographers. Its capacity to use interchangeable lenses makes it extremely flexible and allows the photographer unparalleled scope; constantly evolving, it remains the most versatile of all the camera types.

Below The Asahiflex was one of the earliest SLR cameras, with the same basic design as those available today.

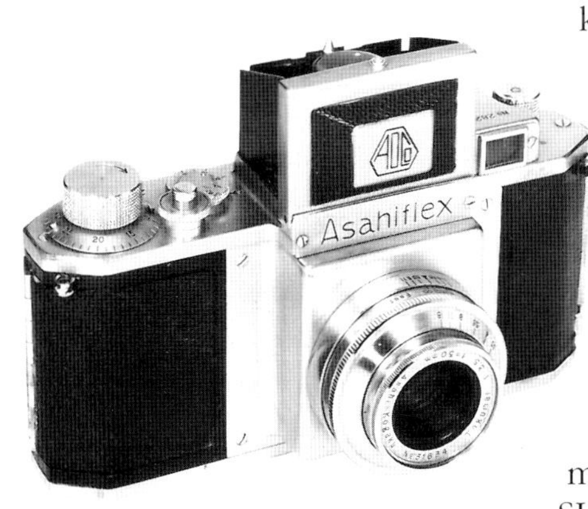

SLRs have been made for many different film formats, ranging from the 110 cartridge to medium-format rollfilm, but by far the most popular is the 35mm format. This book concentrates on the 35mm SLR.

As well as being uniquely versatile, the 35mm interchangeable lens SLR is probably the best camera with which to learn the fundamentals of focusing and exposure. *Essential Camera Skills* explains

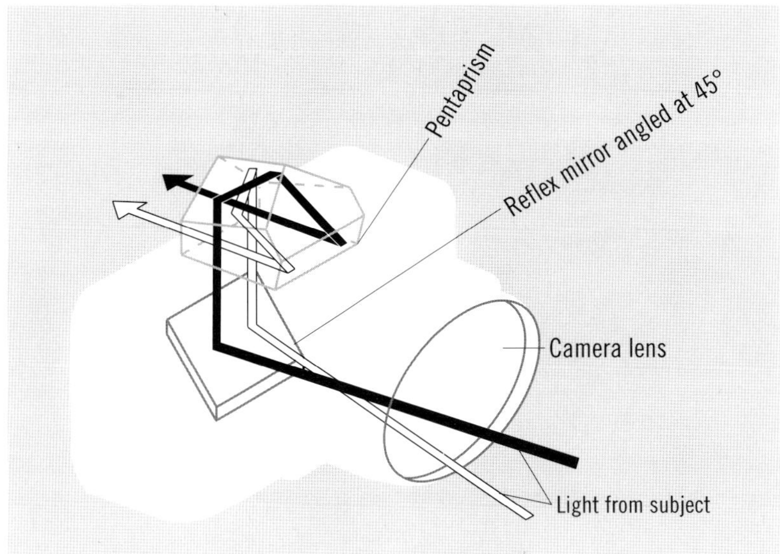

how cameras work, and gives tips and advice on the equipment to use, how best to use it, and the pitfalls to avoid.

It is not just the equipment that counts, though. The book also takes you through the creative side of photography – showing how all the elements of a scene combine to form a balanced picture.

WHAT IS AN SLR?

Viewing When light from the image hits the film in a camera it is the wrong way up and the wrong way round. You can see this for yourself: open an SLR's film back and lock the shutter open, then hold a piece of tracing paper against the film plane, and the image appears on it as it does on the film – upside down and back to front.

Obviously, it is easier to view an image if it is the right way up and the right way round. This is where the pentaprism – the five-sided prism that gives the top of an SLR its distinctive humped

Above The light which hits the film is (when viewed from the back of the camera) the wrong way up and the wrong way round. By bouncing off three surfaces in the pentaprism, the image is back to being the right way round and the right way up when viewed through the viewfinder.

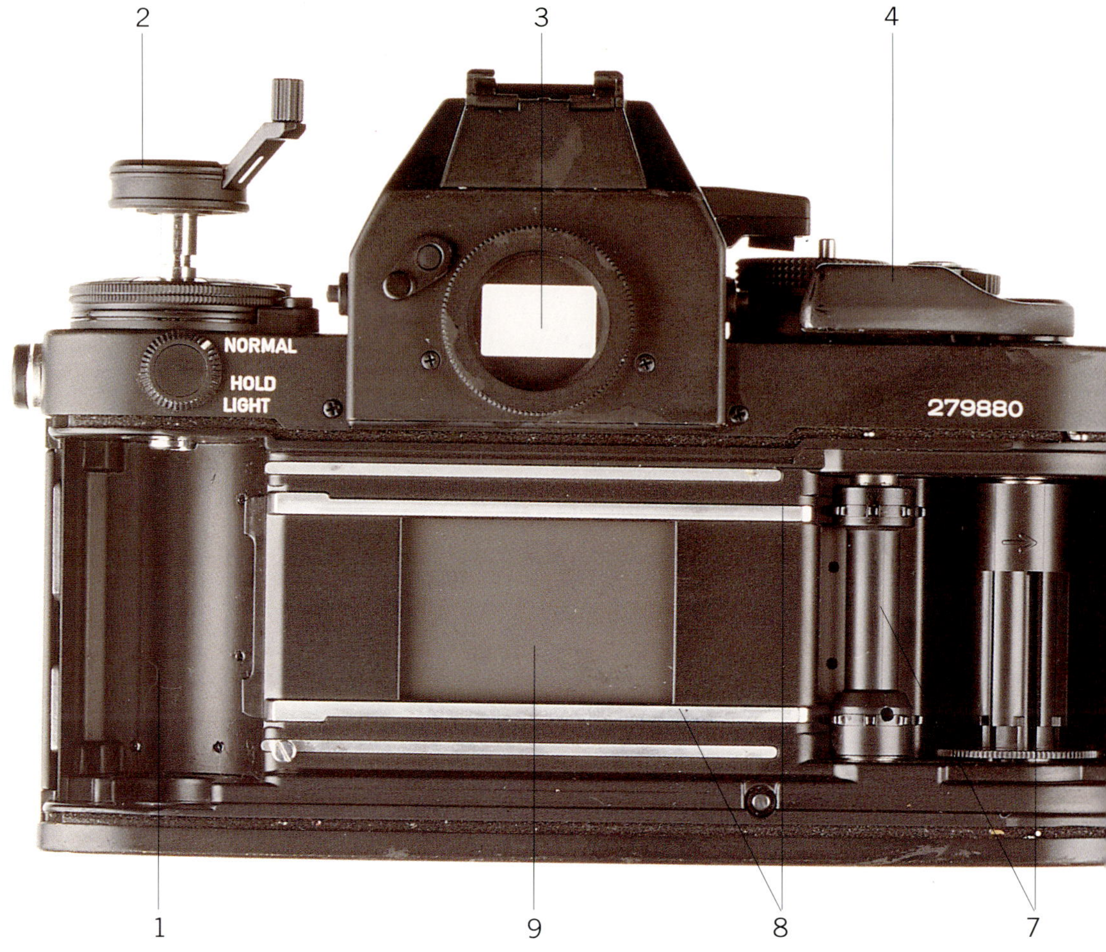

SLR Components

1 film chamber
2 film rewind crank
3 viewfinder eyepiece
4 film wind-on lever
5 film pressure plate
6 film identification window
7 film take-up spool and sprocket
8 film guide rails
9 focal plane shutter
10 depth of field preview
11 camera strap lugs
12 pentaprism housing
13 flash socket
14 finger grip
15 reflex mirror with reflection of focusing screen
16 camera body bayonet fitting
17 lens lock release button: press and then turn lens anticlockwise to remove
18 lens
19 aperture ring
20 shutter speed dial
21 film exposure dial
22 thumb grip
23 flash hotshoe
24 exposure compensation dial
25 memory lock button
26 remote release socket
27 depth of field scale

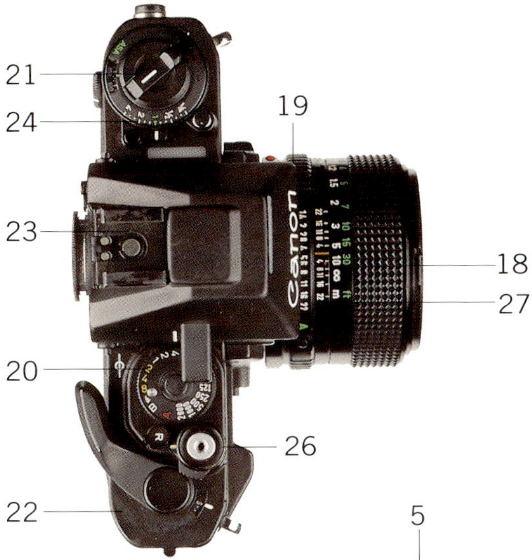

21
24
19
23
18
27
20
26
22
5
6

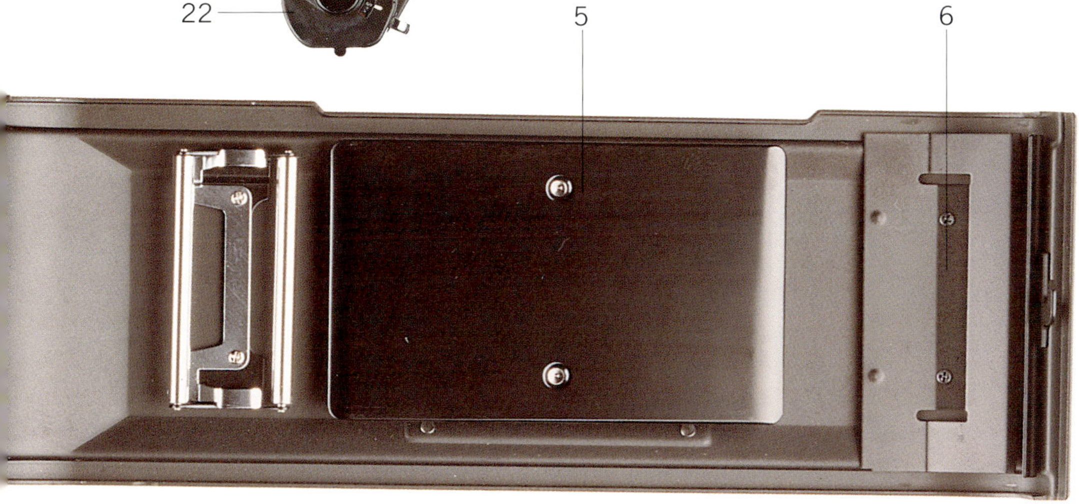

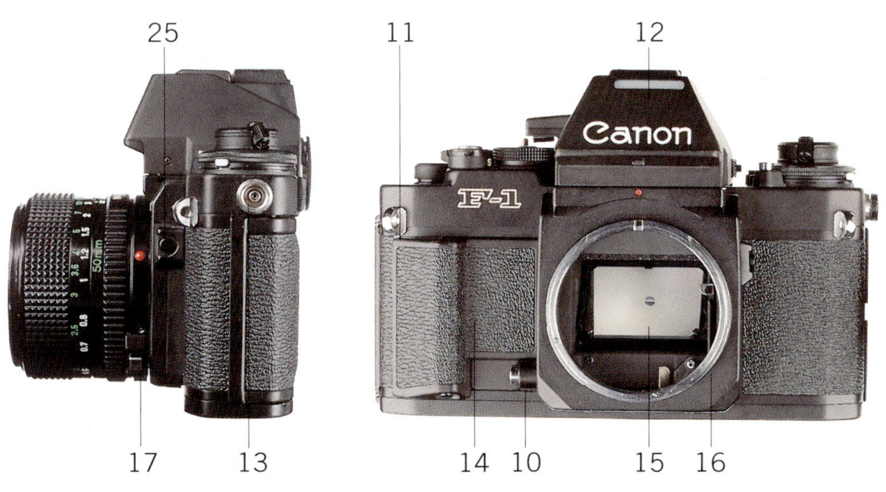
25
11
12
17
13
14
10
15
16

shape – comes into action. The light from the image passes through the lens, strikes the mirror (which laterally reverses the light) and then bounces off all three surfaces in the pentaprism so that when it has passed through the eyepiece it is the correct way round and right way up for accurate and easy viewing.

Between the mirror and the pentaprism is a ground glass screen that is the same distance from the subject as the focal plane is. This screen serves the same purpose as the tracing paper did: it allows the image to be brought to a sharp focus.

A major advantage SLRs have over other types of camera is that much of the information required to take a picture, such as exposure details, can be shown in the viewfinder alongside the image.

Using an SLR Although camera designs are many, there are some tips which apply to all types. Grip the camera in a firm but relaxed way so that the bottom three fingers of the right hand (on the front of the camera) are opposite the thumb (on the back) while the index finger rests lightly and easily on the shutter release. Often the camera has a grip that facilitates this. Supporting the camera's weight like this allows the left hand to operate other features, such as the focusing ring. Keep your elbows into your body and release the shutter smoothly. Jabbing the shutter release can cause camera shake, especially when a slow shutter speed has been set.

Film advance 35mm film is edged with sprocket holes – showing its origins as a movie film stock – allowing it to be advanced quickly. Cameras either have a built-in motor which advances the film after each exposure, or a manual wind-on lever. The film is held flat against a pair of rails by a sprung pressure plate on the inside of the back of the camera. If both rails and plate are not absolutely clean,

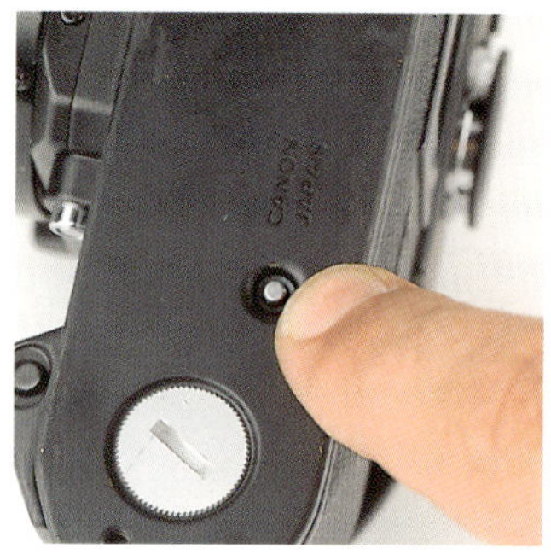

Above and below To rewind, first press rewind button ... then gently turn rewind crank until the film is wound back (when there is no resistance to turning).

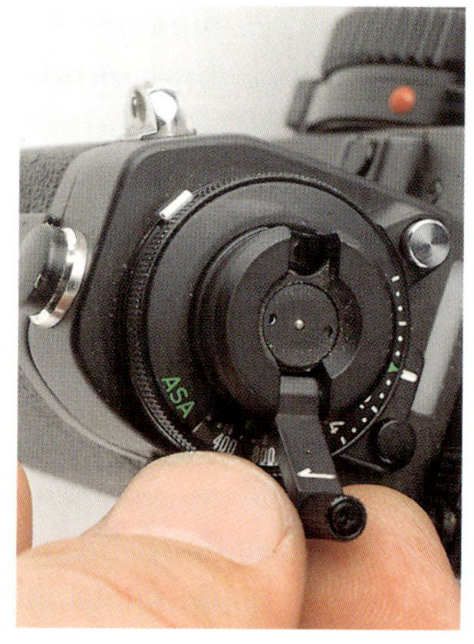

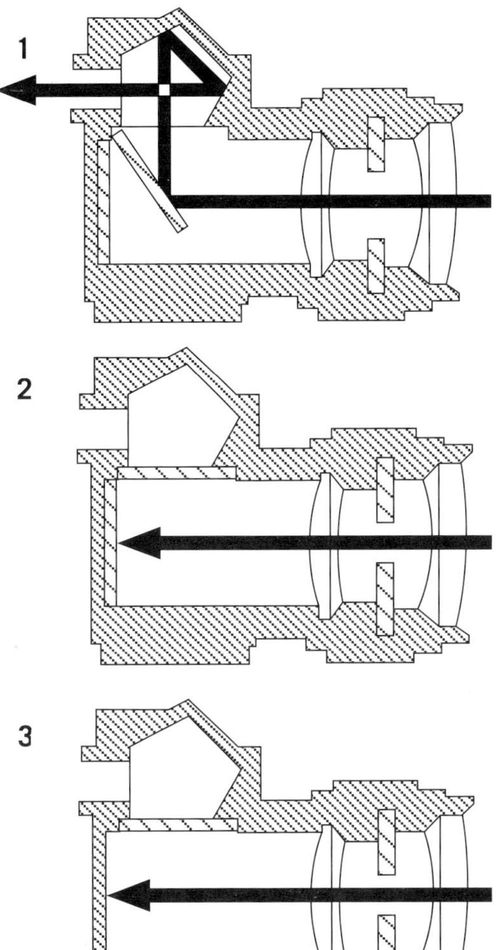

or are damaged, the film may be scratched or not completely flat. In the latter case, there is a chance that your pictures will not be sharp.

When the film comes to its end, it is either rewound by a motor or manually, by turning a crank. In the case of the camera shown on the left, you turn the crank clockwise while pressing the rewind button on the base plate of the camera (this button releases the lock on the film sprockets – if it is not released the film could rip).

With a manual rewind camera, always check that the crank moves anticlockwise when you advance the film. If it does not, it means one of three things: there is no film in the camera, the film is ripped, or the film is not wound on properly.

How film is exposed An SLR has three states, as the diagrams show.

1 The first is the viewing state. The reflex mirror is down, allowing the photographer to see the scene.

2 After the shutter is pressed, the mirror is raised; at the same time the lens aperture closes from its open position to the chosen setting.

3 Once this has happened, the shutter opens and the film is exposed.

At the end of the exposure the shutter closes, the lens opens up to its maximum aperture and the mirror swings back down into position for viewing as in diagram 1. This takes only a fraction of a second, but because of the speed of movement, unless the camera is firmly held the vibration could cause the picture to be slightly blurred.

The Lens

There are few differences between most lenses in terms of what components they contain. They are all made up of glass elements and a mechanical system that positions these elements so the image can be brought to sharp focus.

As well as the focusing mechanism and optical elements, nearly all lenses have a diaphragm, which is basically a hole of variable size that controls the amount of light hitting the film plane. This variation in the size of the hole is achieved by using between six and eight curved metallic blades (see diagram, left) mechanically controlled by an 'aperture' ring on the lens, or through a button or dial on the camera. Pre-set increments for the aperture – known as f-stops – are marked on the aperture ring.

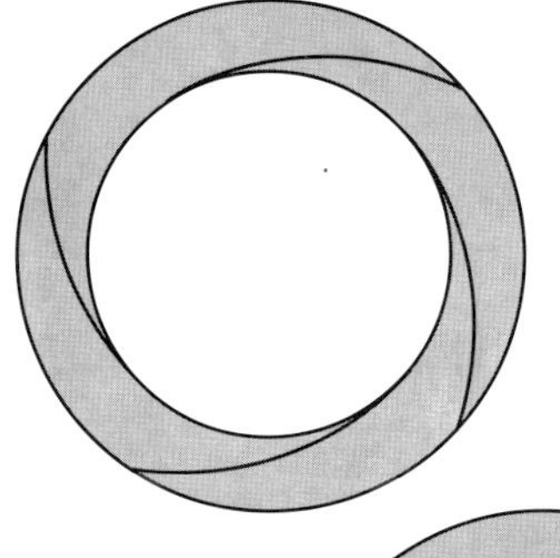

Top
Full aperture

Bottom
Stopped down

Apart from the aperture ring, most SLR lenses also have a focusing ring which allows the photographer to adjust the relative positions of the optical elements. Some lenses also have a depth of field scale.

The rear of the lens houses the lens mount, which enables lenses to be fixed onto the appropriate camera. On most lens mounts there is an aperture lever which is attached to a spring inside the lens. This spring keeps the diaphragm blades stopped down. When the lens is put on the camera body, a lever in the body marries up against the spring so that the diaphragm is kept fully open for bright viewing and focusing. At the moment of exposure, the lever moves out of the way, and the lens's aperture spring closes the diaphragm down to the set aperture. This lever also moves out of the way if the camera's depth of field preview is used.

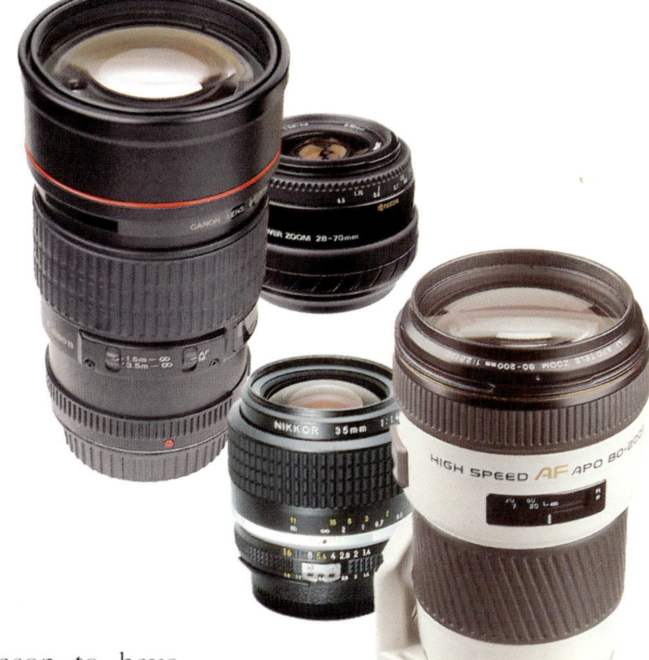

Right Lenses come in all shapes and sizes, from mammoth telephoto (bottom right) to wideangle zoom (centre top). In general the bigger the front element, the more expensive the lens.

Focal length The main reason to have interchangeable lenses is to be able to use different focal lengths. The focal length of a lens (which is given in millimetres) is an indicator of its enlarging power. The higher the figure, the bigger the magnification. With an SLR (using 35mm film) the lens that approximates the magnification of the human eye has a focal length of 50mm.

The flipside of magnification is field – or angle – of view; how much you can fit into the frame (see diagram overleaf). The smaller the focal length, the wider the field of view, hence the term 'wideangle'. Longer focal lengths allow you to shoot distant subjects while still keeping a reasonable image size, and are known as telephoto.

Lens types Most lenses are refractors – light benders. The amount the light is bent depends on the curvature of the lens, and the bending

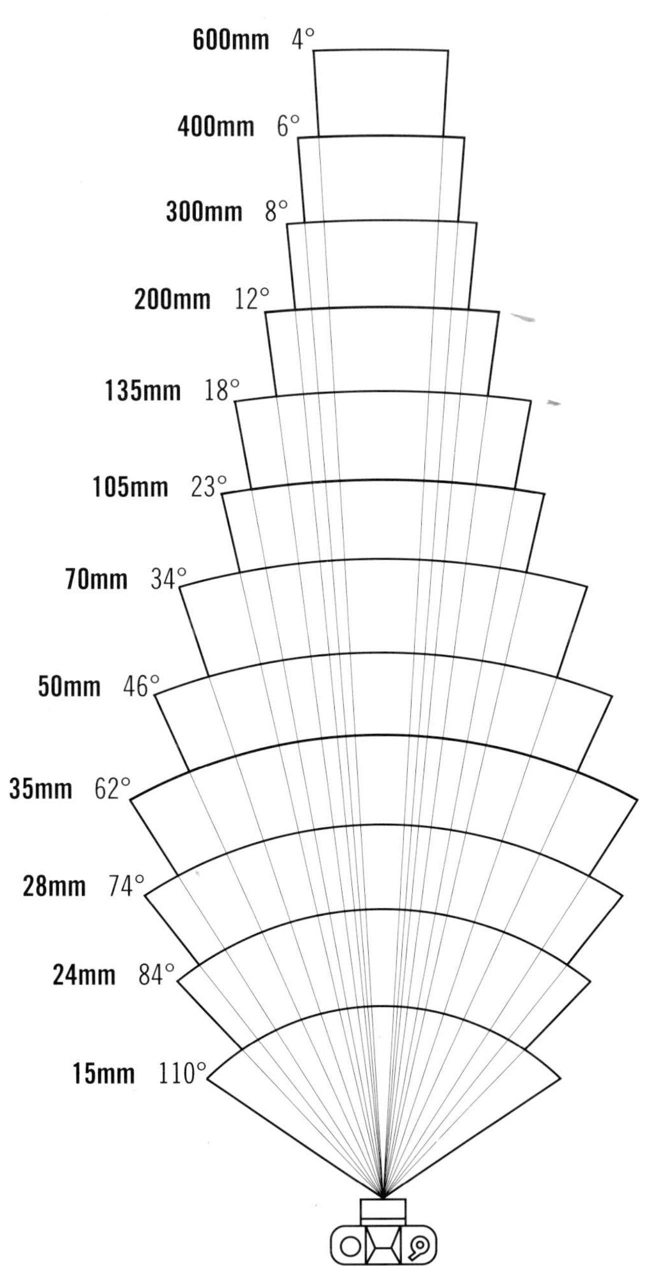

Above Focal lengths and angles of view.

Right This series of shots shows the difference in image magnification and field of view obtainable with different lenses from the same position. The lenses used have focal lengths from a 15mm fisheye (so called for the bending distortion at the edges of the frame) through to a 600mm telephoto. To realize the full nature of the difference in magnification involved, try to pick out the clock face in the 15mm shot – it is at the centre of the picture!

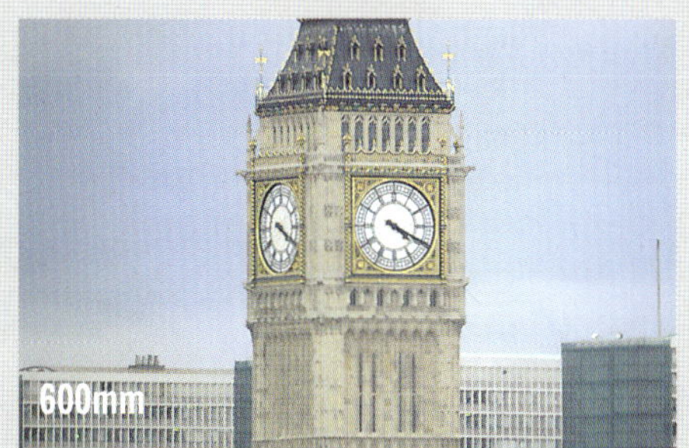
600mm

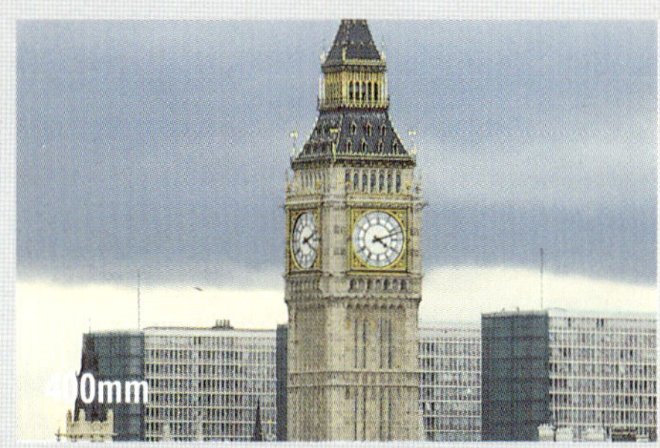
400mm

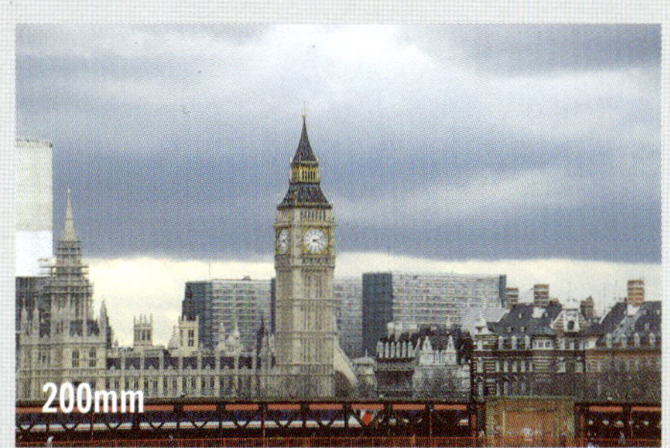
200mm

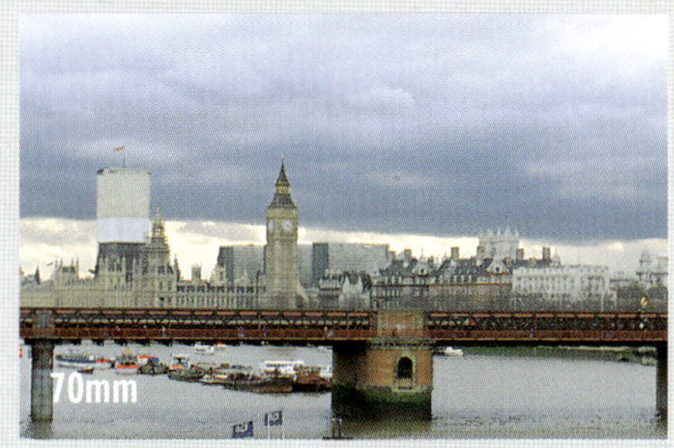
70mm

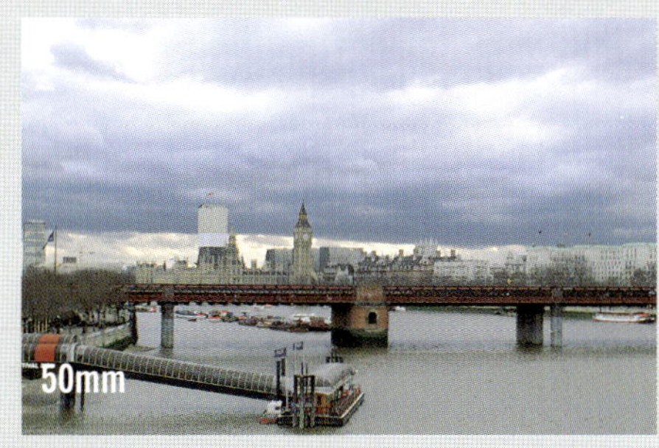
50mm

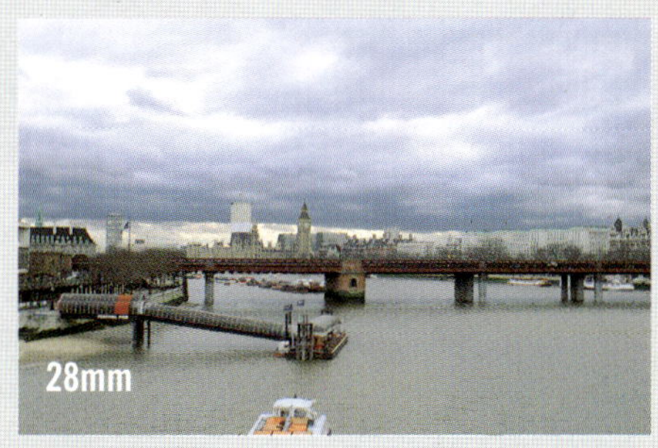
28mm

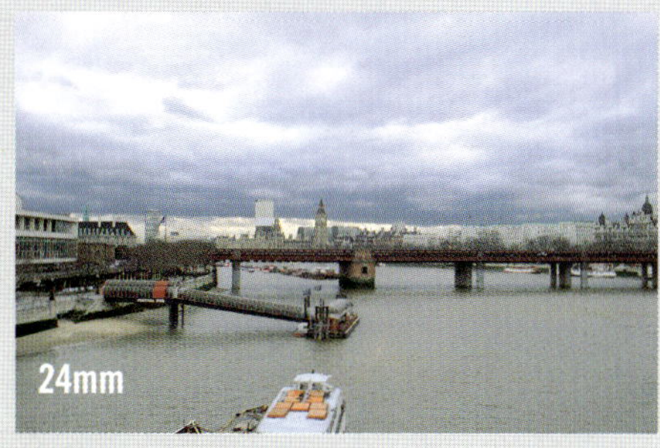
24mm

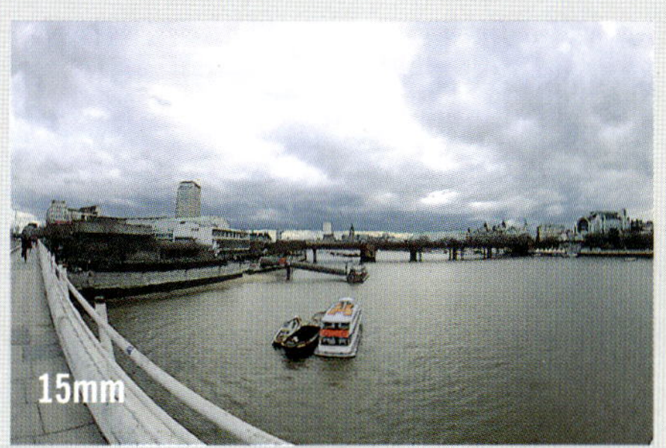
15mm

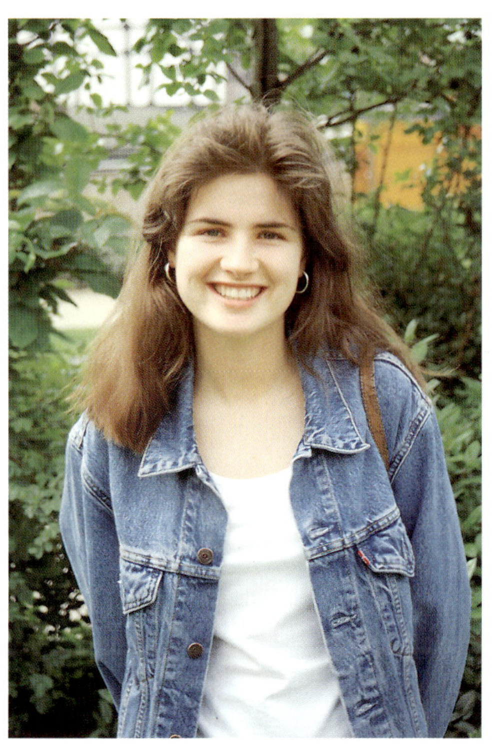

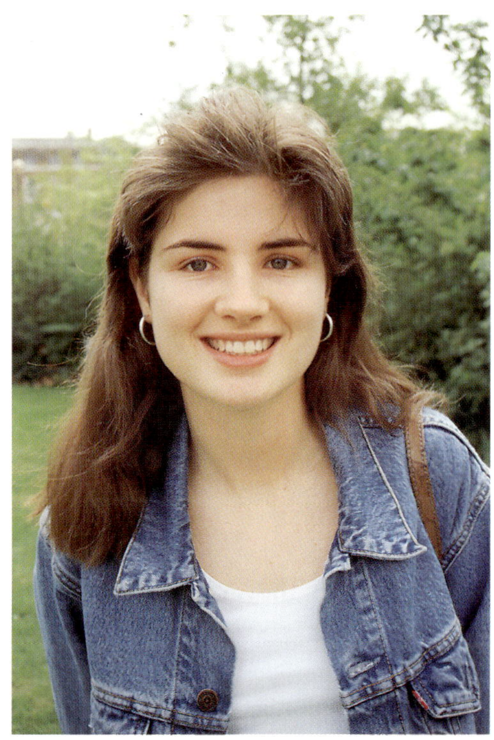

power of the glass. Wideangle lenses bend light most, and their front elements are more noticeably curved than telephotos.

Some lenses use not only refraction but also reflections to bring the image onto the film. These are known as mirror or catadioptric lenses. Their main advantage is that they allow telephoto lenses, which can be unwieldy, to be constructed much shorter. Mirror lenses also have a fixed aperture rather than a variable one.

Lenses do not have to have a single focal length. Variable focal length lenses (zooms) have become more widely available in the last few years. Zooms are often referred to as 2x or 3x types. This factor is the maximum focal length over the minimum focal length – ie a 75–300mm zoom would be a 4x zoom (300/75x).

Above and right Perspective is very important in portraiture as it can be used to 'de-emphasize' or exaggerate facial features. The shots here were taken on 15mm, 35mm and 300mm lenses at shooting distances of 30cm, 70cm and 6m respectively. Which picture would you prefer if you were the subject?

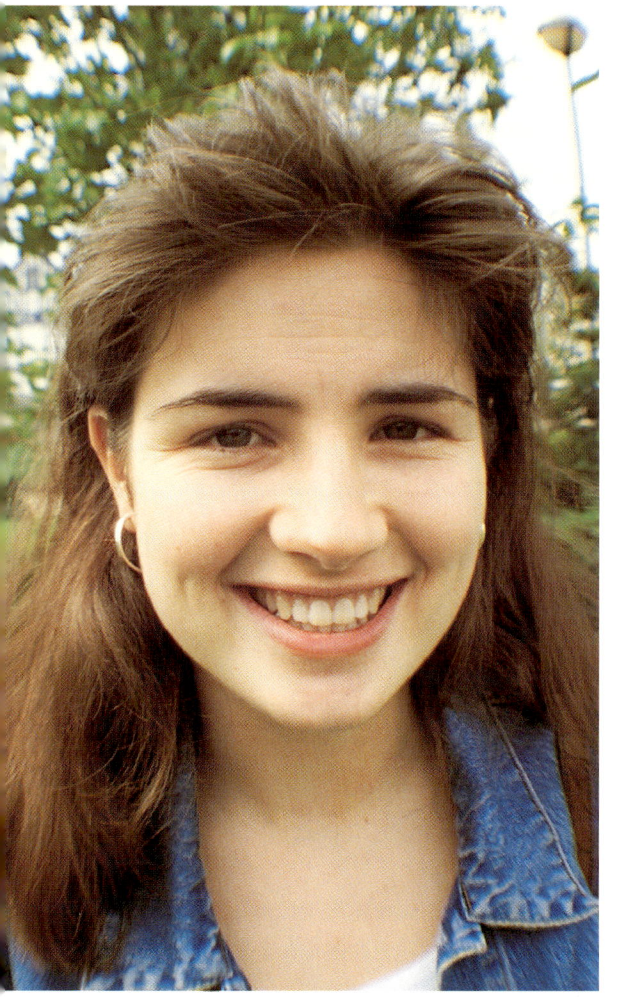

Perspective Perspective is not a function of the lens you are using, but its effects are most visible when using different lenses. The distance you are from a subject and its distance from the background is what determines their relative sizes – their perspective.

If your subject is close and its background distant, then the subject will look much larger in relation to the background than it really is. If the subject is distant, the background looks bigger than it should. If you use only a 50mm lens, chances are that this effect will not look strange as the human brain subconsciously uses it relative subject size to calculate distance anyway. It is only when using very wide or very long lenses that perspective changes become obvious.

If you use a wideangle lens close to a subject, the image size of the subject in relation to the background appears disproportionate. Using a long lens with a distant subject will magnify the background so the subject looks smaller than it should. This effect is known as compressed perspective. Using a wideangle lens close to a portrait subject will make the sitter's nose large and bulbous, the ears tiny and almost on the back of an enormous head, and the shoulders narrow. Keeping the same image size but moving further away flattens the perspective, giving more attractively proportioned features, broader shoulders and a smaller head.

Shutter and Exposure

The shutter All interchangeable lens 35mm SLRs use the same type of shutter: the focal plane twin blind system, more commonly known as the focal plane shutter (due to the fact that it is positioned just in front of the film plane). The principle behind it is simple.

When the film is wound on, the shutter mechanism is cocked and ready to fire. At this stage, one of the blinds is covering the path between the lens and film, the other poised to travel across that path. When the shutter release button is pressed,

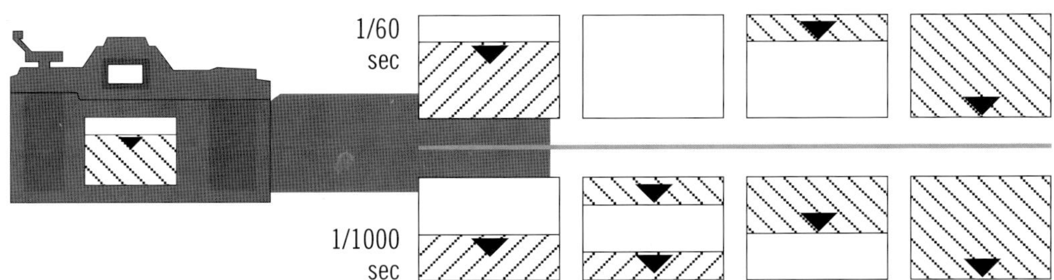

Above The four stages of exposure with a focal plane shutter, showing the difference between 1/60sec (top), when the film is exposed completely, and 1/1000sec (bottom), when the film is exposed by a strip of light passing over it.

the blind blocking the light opens (in most cameras moving from top to bottom), then the second blind moves down to cover the path again. As the diagram above shows, for long shutter speeds (1/60sec and slower), the first blind completes its journey before the second starts to move. With faster shutter speeds, the blinds physically cannot move fast enough, so the film is effectively exposed by a moving strip. The fastest speed at which the first blind stops moving before the second starts is known as the maximum flash synchronization speed.

Exposure Three factors affect the amount of light hitting the film. The first is the light level of the scene you are photographing. The second and third, over which you have the most control, are the aperture and shutter speed you choose.

Open up the aperture (bigger hole, smaller f-number), and more light hits the film. Close down the aperture (smaller hole, bigger f-number), and less light hits the film. The longer the shutter speed, the more light hits the film, and the shorter the shutter speed, the less light hits it. One click up or down the range of shutter speeds doubles or halves the length of the exposure. Changing aperture by one click (or 'stop') either way doubles or halves the amount of light hitting the film.

Increasing the shutter speed by one click (say, from 1/60 to 1/125sec) and decreasing (opening up) the aperture by one stop should give the same overall exposure. This is known as the reciprocity law, and is most easily understandable if you think of an exposure as a cylindrical volume of light. The aperture is the area of light passing through

Below The reciprocity law: all the shutter speed/aperture combinations shown give the same exposure. The exposure is represented as a cylindrical volume of light.

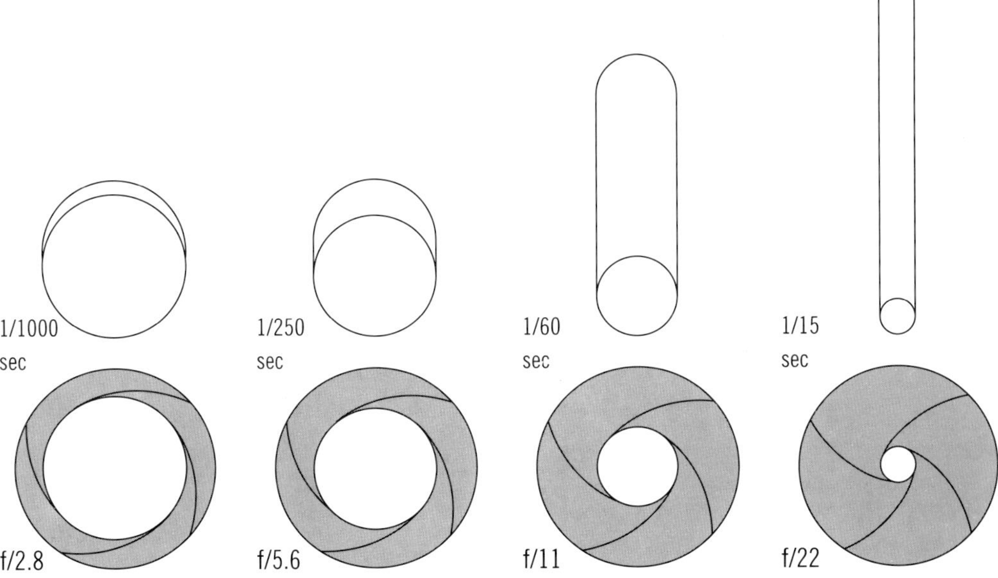

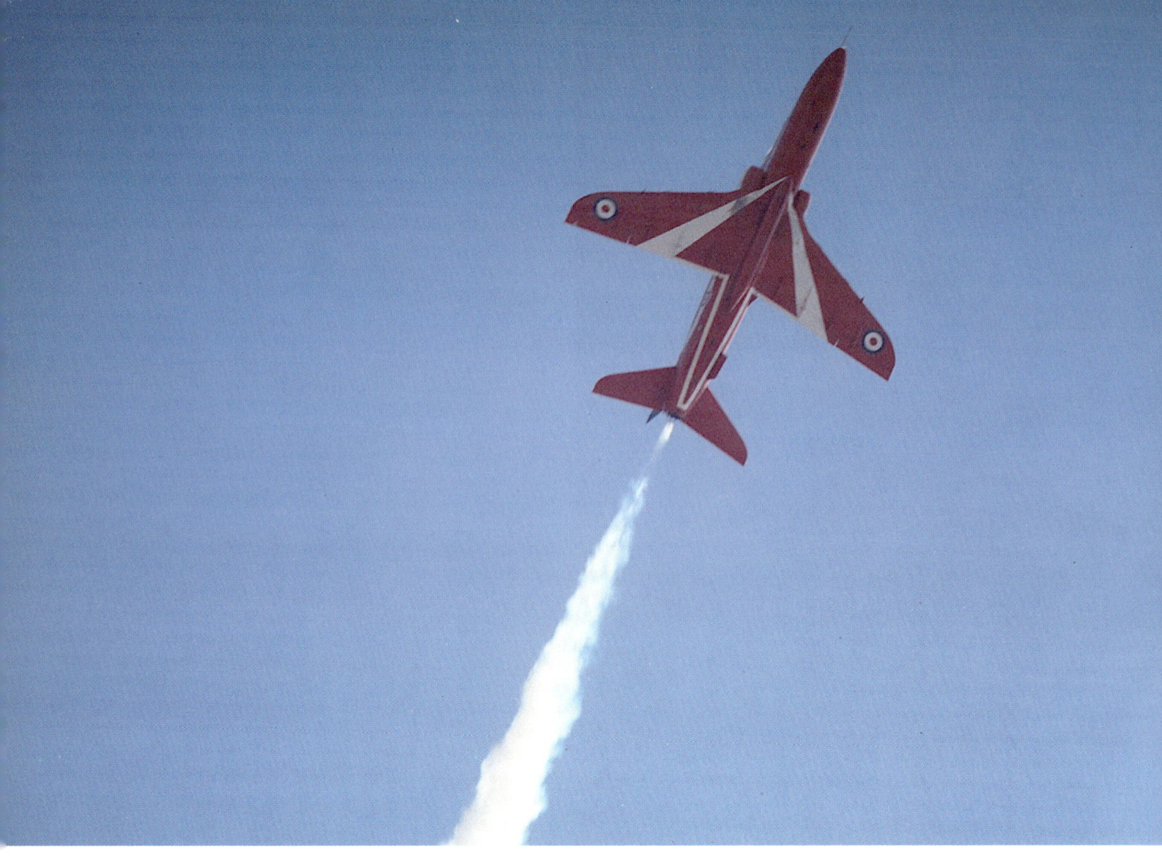

Above Fast shutter speeds – 1/500 sec and above – can be used to freeze such ultra-fast subjects as the Red Arrows.

the lens, and the shutter speed defines the length of the cylinder. Multiply one by the other and you get the volume of light: its exposure value.

There are two other considerations affecting exposure: the sensitivity of the film being used (see pages 24–7), and the amount of light coming into the camera (see pages 28–33).

F-stops Apertures are numbered in f-stops – usually somewhere in the following range: 1.4, 2, 2.8, 4, 5.6, 8, 11, 16, 22, 32, 45. The f-stop is the ratio of focal length to the diameter of the hole – f/2 on a 50mm lens is a 25mm (50/2) hole. An increase in the diameter of the aperture by a factor of 1.4 doubles the area of the aperture, and this doubles the amount of light coming through the lens. This why aperture numbers double only every two stops. As stated, f-stops are a ratio: a 200mm lens at f/8 will let the same amount of light through the lens onto the film as a 20mm lens at f/8.

Fast or slow Apart from adjusting the shutter speed to suit an aperture selected for a particular depth of field, it is also possible to change a scene by altering the shutter speed. If you choose a short shutter speed (1/250sec or faster) it is likely that all the elements in a scene will be frozen. The longer the shutter speed used, the more likely it is that a moving subject will be blurred. Such blurring can convey an impression of speed more successfully than the static image from a short shutter speed. But there is also the risk that the photographer may have moved slightly during the whole exposure – meaning that the whole shot, not just the moving subject, will come out blurred unless the camera is held still. To be on the safe side, try not to use a shutter speed slower than 1/30sec when handholding the camera.

The longer the focal length of the lens, the faster the shutter speed required to eliminate camera shake. A guideline is that the shutter speed should not be slower than 1/(focal length) of the lens you are using – for example 1/500sec for a 500mm lens, 1/125sec for a 100mm lens and so on. For really long exposures (usually at night), most cameras have a bulb or B setting. On this setting, the shutter stays open for as long as the

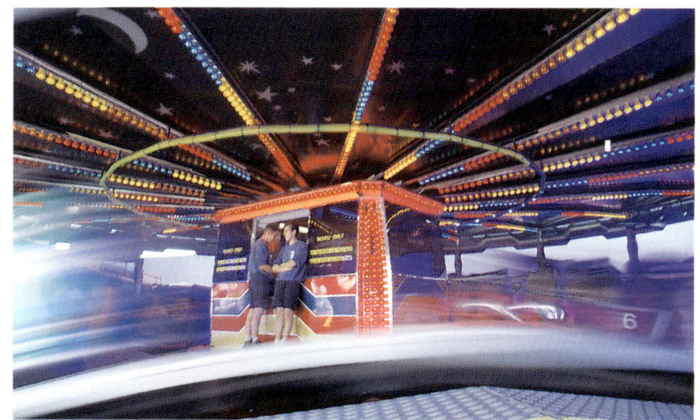

Left By using a slow shutter speed, it is possible to 'ghost' the edge of moving subjects while the centre scene is perfectly still. This shot used a 1/15sec exposure.

shutter release is depressed. Its name hails from the days of the early pneumatic shutter releases.

Automatic cameras When using a camera that has neither manual aperture nor shutter speed control, your initial impression may be that there is little chance of getting the right exposure in a tricky lighting situation. This is further compounded because cameras of this type are also unlikely to indicate what exposure they have taken. Fortunately, if you know the situations in which the camera will get it wrong, it is easy to override it.

The first step is to use a film that has a relatively high ISO speed and a wide latitude. Colour or mono ISO 400 print film is best. The reason for choosing a film with wide latitude (ie print film) is so that if the camera does get it wrong, there is a fighting chance that the film will still register a useable image. The reason for making it a fast film is because print films react much better to being overexposed (getting too much light) than being underexposed. Underexposed films tend to look very grainy and their colours desaturated (greyish). Most modern colour print film overexposed by up to three stops will still produce better results than those underexposed by one stop.

Below This shot, showing panning at 1/250sec, has little background movement.

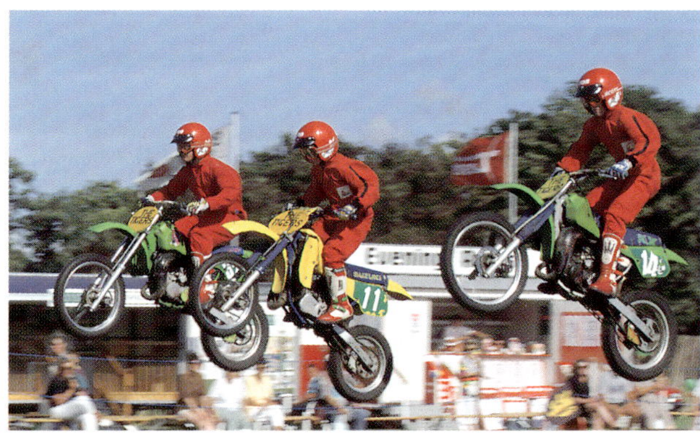

If your camera has a tendency to under- or overexpose in specific conditions, and you plan on shooting in those conditions, you can re-rate the film to compensate. Cameras that are predominantly automatic will not allow you to do this, so the best option is to use the DX recoder (see page 24). If, say, your camera tends to underexpose by a couple of stops, load an ISO 400 film with an

ISO 100 recoder over the DX contacts, and the two-stop overexposure caused by this should neutralize the camera's tendency to underexpose.

While this system is adequate for whole film mistakes, it takes no account of single shots where you know the camera will go wrong but you do not want to unload and reload a film with a recoder on it, only to unload and remove the recoder and so on. If you want to make the camera give more exposure to the film than it ordinarily would, place a neutral density (ND) filter of known strength over the light-sensitive sensor, fooling the camera into thinking there is less light around than there actually is, and therefore into giving a longer exposure. A 2x ND filter will give you one stop more exposure, a 4x ND two stops more and so on.

Below This picture, showing panning at 1/60sec, really shows 'action' to the viewer.

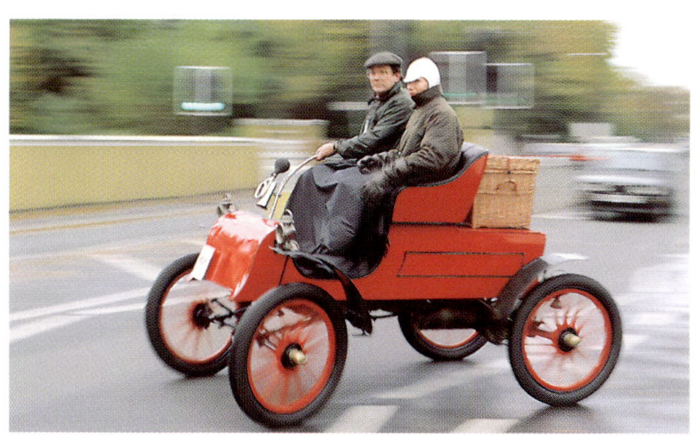

The ND filter also allows you to compensate for overexposure problems. If your camera is likely to overexpose a scene (say, a small subject in front of a black wall), place the ND filter over the lens but not the exposure sensor.

If you have an SLR with an automatic exposure (AE) lock, find an object of the correct tone (ie mid-grey) in the same light as your subject, lock the exposure on it and then recompose the shot. If the exposure and focusing on your camera are both locked by a half-pressure on the shutter release, find a mid-toned subject at the same distance from the camera as the main subject is going to be. If this is not possible, move so that the mid-toned subject is the same distance from the camera as the main subject will be when you return to the spot from which you wish to take the picture.

The Film

All films share the same basic composition: a scratch-resistant coating on top of the emulsion layer(s), then an anti-halation layer – which stops light bouncing back through the emulsion a second time – and a film base that strengthens the other layers (see diagram).

Black and white (monochrome) negative film is the simplest form of film in widespread use. It is called negative film because after development the film forms an image that is opposite in tonal terms to the original view. White objects become black, light tones appear dark grey and blacks are clear on the negative.

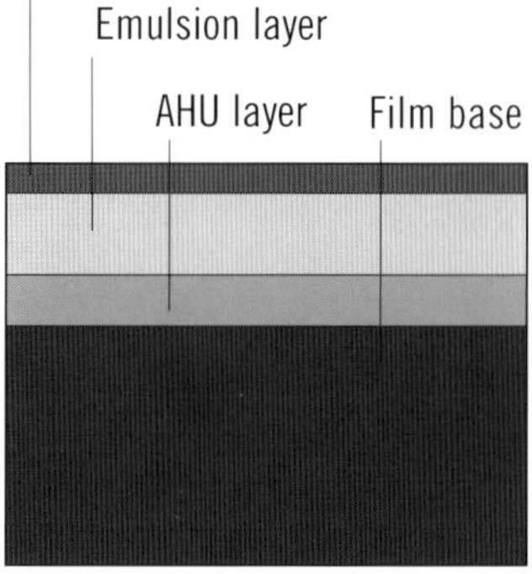

Above This section of Agfapan 25 monochrome film shows the basic construction of a slow monochrome film.

Below A glance at a film box will tell you all you need to know.

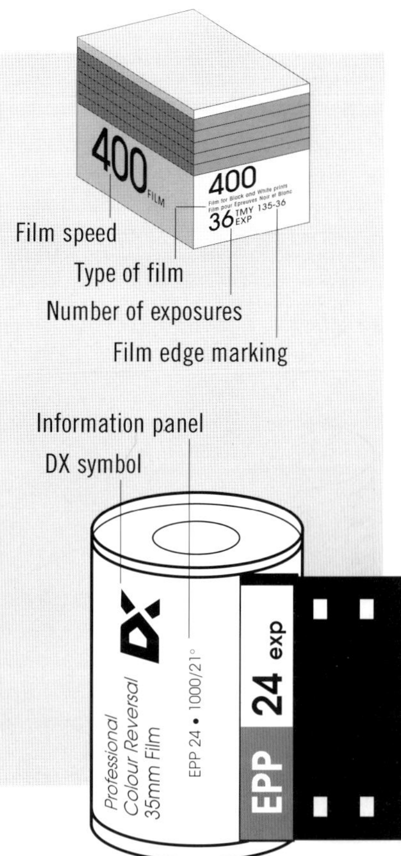

Film speed and DX coding Apart from the prevalent level of light and the aperture and shutter speed in use, the variable that determines whether a correct exposure is made is the sensitivity of the film to light: its speed.

Film speed is given in terms of an ISO rating (formerly known as ASA), and works in the same doubling/halving method as the other exposure variables. For example, a film of speed ISO 100 is twice as sensitive as a film of ISO 50, and requires half the exposure to get the same result. Most films fall in the ISO range 25–3200, with ISO 25 being the least sensitive of that range and ISO 3200 the most sensitive.

Most modern cameras use a system called DX coding to set the film speed automatically when a film is loaded. A set of contacts on the inside of the camera electrically 'reads' a chequerboard arrangement of silver and black squares on the film canister. More expensive cameras allow this automatically set film speed to be overridden by the user, while older models have only manual setting.

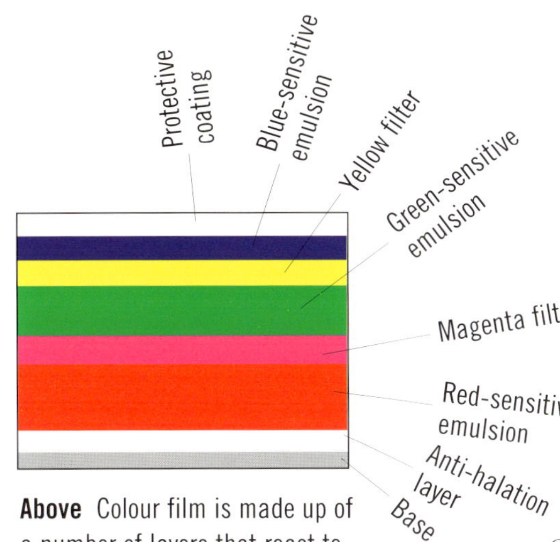

Above Colour film is made up of a number of layers that react to different colours of light.

Colour negative film (also known as colour print) works on much the same principle, except that instead of the tones being reversed, the colours are theoretically opposite to those in the original scene. Rather than one emulsion layer, there are three – one sensitive to each of the primary colours of light (red, green and blue). Colour negative films show an orange cast after they have been developed.

Transparency (slide) film uses much the same system as colour negative film, except that at the development stage the negative image is bleached out and then replaced by a positive image by an extra stage in the process – hence its alternative name 'reversal film'.

Reading film Both film canisters and boxes are loaded with information about what kind of film is inside. Knowing what a film does allows you to make the right decision as to which type to use for any given circumstance.

The canister is also host to information for the film processor, whose machines can read barcodes not only on the canister, but also on the edge of the film once it has been developed. Each type of colour print film has a different filtration requirement during printing because the background cast is not the same for all films. Larger processing companies have separate 'channels' – filtration set-ups – for various films, and being able automatically to identify a film allows their printing machines to

Camera autosensing code detailed below

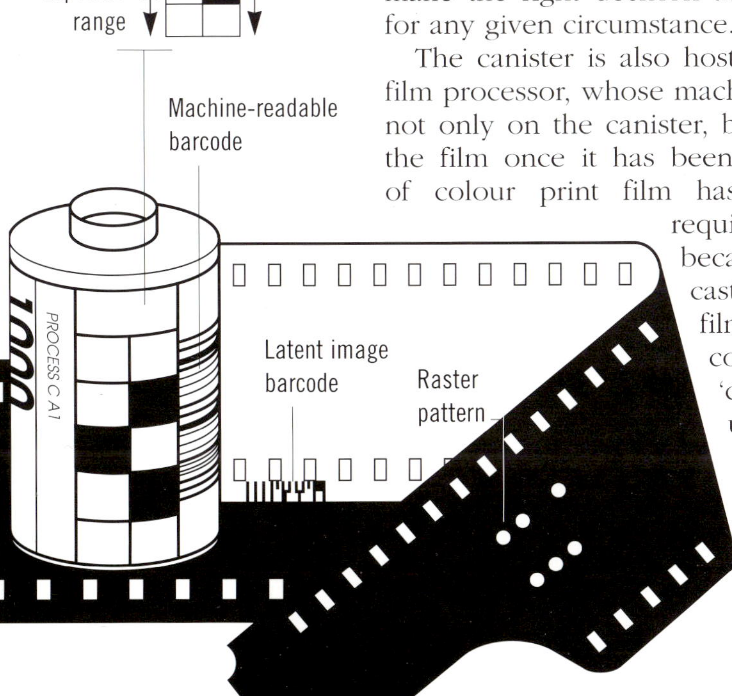

give the correct filtration for any given type of print film.

Grain The emulsion of a film is made up of light-sensitive particles suspended in gelatin. The larger the surface area of these particles, the more sensitive they are to light and the faster the film (the higher the ISO number). When photographs are greatly enlarged, it is possible to see the particles, or grains. The larger the grain size, the less detail the film can resolve. The bigger the enlargement made of a print the more evident the grain will be.

Below Looking at these two images, it is plain to see the price paid in grain size for the bottom picture's ISO 3200 speed compared to the ISO 100 shot on the top.

Film choice So what kind of film should you choose? As with most things, the answer is 'it depends'. Two basic decisions need to be made: which type of film – black and white, colour print, colour transparency – is most suitable; and which speed is needed.

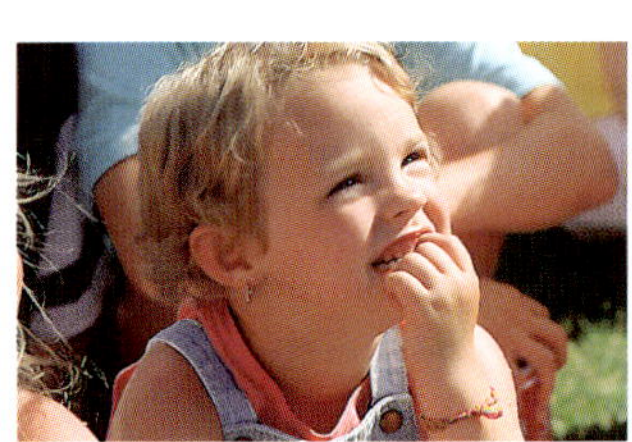

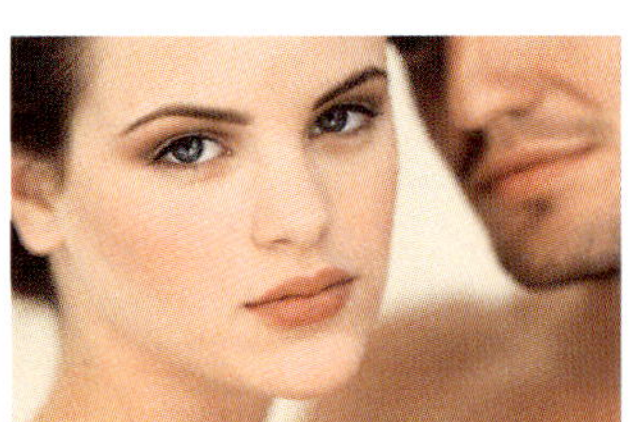

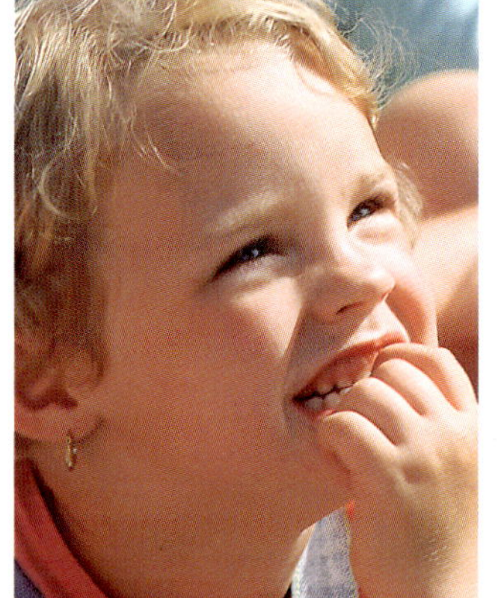

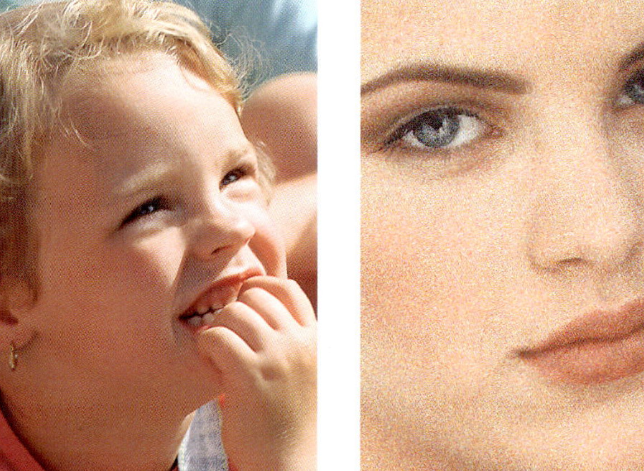

In terms of quality, a good transparency is better than a good colour print, but it has limitations in how it can be presented. Prints from transparencies are certainly possible, but tend to be expensive compared to printing prices for negatives. If colour is not the most important item in a scene, black and white is the best choice, especially as processing and printing monochrome pictures yourself gives you ultimate control over your finished pictures.

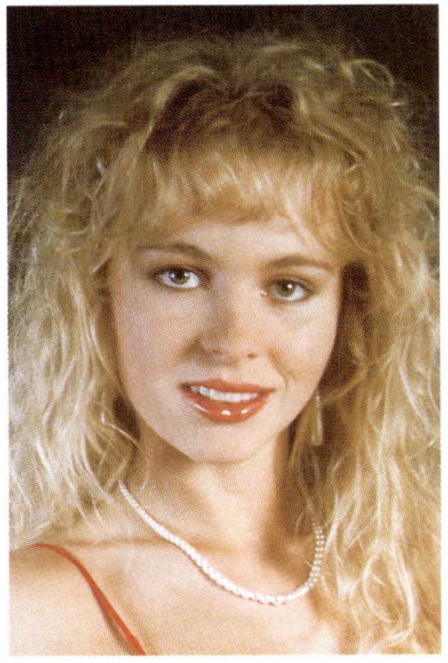

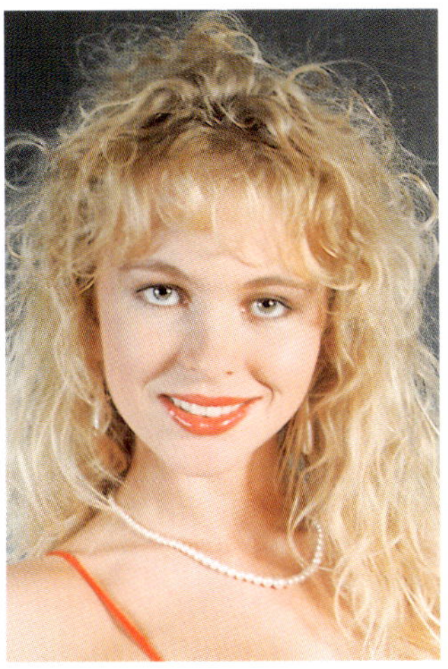

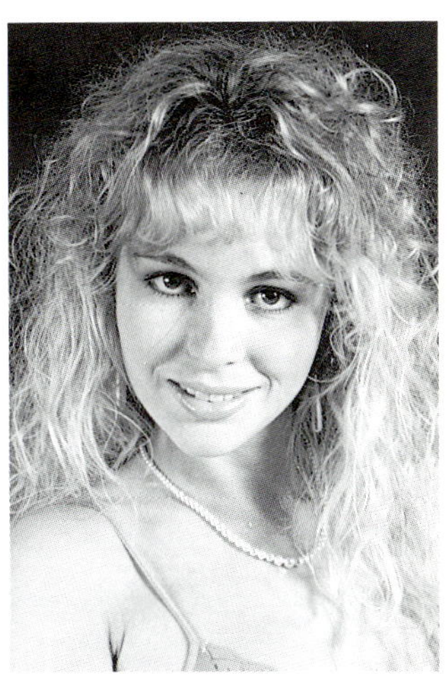

Above These three pictures taken (from left to right) on Kodak Gold 100 print film, Fuji Velvia slide film and Kodak Technical Pan mono film, show how different films reproduce the same scene. Note the brighter colours and higher contrast of the slide shot compared to the print film shot.

When choosing which speed of film you need, a good rule of thumb is that the meter should recommend a shutter speed/aperture combination of 1/125sec at f/8 (or any equivalent exposure) for an average subject in the available light, with your chosen film. If you choose a fast film (say ISO 1000) when there is too much light, you will be restricted to using small apertures (such as f/16) and fast shutter speed (for instance 1/1000sec). Although this is fine for sharp pictures, it allows no creative manipulation of depth of field.

Choosing a slow film such as ISO 25 in low light is worse, as you will be obliged to use a slow shutter speed (for example 1/4sec) with a strong risk of camera shake, and a wide aperture (such as f/2) that gives virtually no depth of field.

Selecting a film that puts you slap-bang in the middle of the exposure range (say 1/125sec at f/8) also gives you a bit of insurance against changing light levels in variable weather.

Metering

Having discussed how the three other elements of exposure – shutter speed, aperture and film speed – work, we are now going to look at the amount of light that reaches the camera and how the camera measures it.

The meters built into an SLR are known as direct or reflected light meters. The way the meter of a very simple camera sees the world is by assuming that it is looking at a scene that will reflect an average of 18 per cent of the light falling on it. This 18 per cent reflectance corresponds to a mid-tone grey.

The meter recommends an exposure that will reproduce this mid-tone exactly for a given light level. In bright light the meter will recommend a shorter shutter speed and smaller aperture (say 1/250sec at f/16); low light will require a longer shutter speed and wider aperture (say 1/4sec at f/2).

The obvious problem is that the world is not a uniform mid-tone grey. But, as the meter's standard is a mid-tone, a combination of highly reflective and very dull subjects should average out at a mid-tone and allow the meter to gauge the light level correctly.

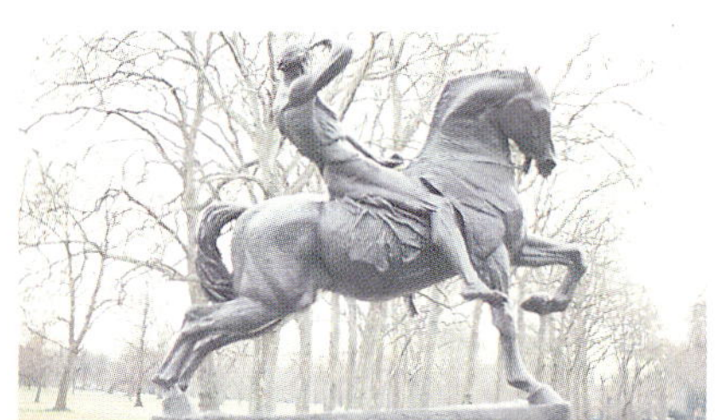

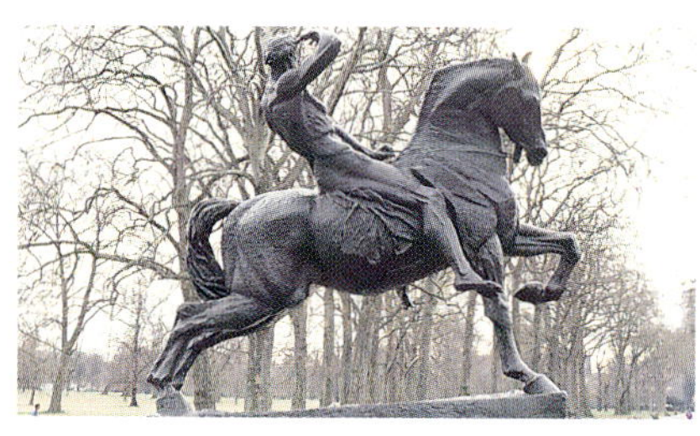

Above With mainly black subjects, the meter gets it wrong (top) without compensation (bottom).

Negative and positive How under- and overexposure appear on a developed film or print depends on the type of film. On a slide or print, a very light image denotes overexposure, while underexposure gives a dark result. With a negative, a very dense look indicates overexposure, while a thin neg has received too little light. With negative film, plus or minus two stops of exposure is usually correctable at the printing stage; slide film cannot be rescued after development.

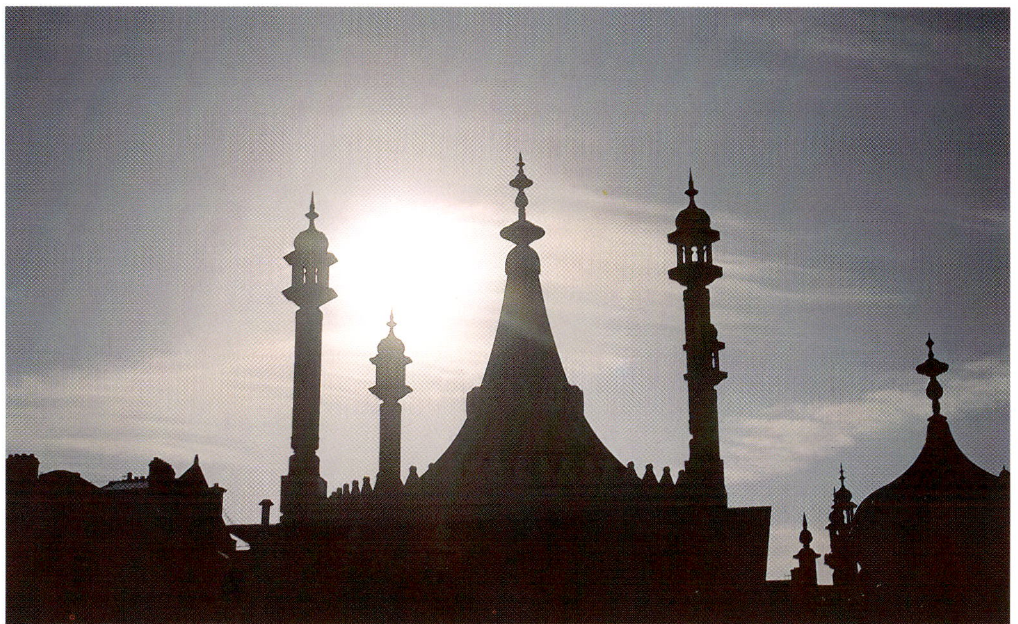

Above To get a silhouette picture simply point the meter at the sky and expose.

Looking at pictures with incorrect exposure is the best way of learning about exposure, as you can see when the meter is fooled.

Reading a scene As camera meters assume they are looking at a mid-tone scene when calculating light levels, if you point a camera at a white wall and use the recommended exposure, you will end up with a grey wall. Similarly, if you have a very dark subject and expose according to the meter's recommendation, you will get a grey result.

So when exposing a picture, always be aware of parts of the scene that will fool the meter. If the sun is in the frame, for example, it will cause the meter to set a shutter speed and aperture that will underexpose the film, giving silhouettes.

The way around this is to try to find something in the scene that is both mid-tone and receiving the same amount of light as your main subject; paving stones are very often a good bet. Set your shutter speed and aperture according to the meter's recommendations for that mid-tone, then recompose the shot and take the picture. There are two alternatives to this if there is no adequate mid-tone in the scene.

The first is to carry a grey card around with you (available from photographic shops) that reflects back precisely 18 per cent of the light falling on it. Place the card next to the subject and set the exposure according to the meter's recommendation for the card.

The second alternative is exposure compensation. If a scene takes up a relatively large portion of your total shot and is lighter than a mid-tone, then left to its own devices the meter will underexpose. To expose the scene correctly, override the meter's recommendation and set a shutter speed and aperture that will give one to two stops (depending on the scene) more exposure.

Below With the sun just out of the frame, try metering from the lower part of the scene by shielding the top of the lens with your hand. Be sure to leave a bit of the sky in the frame.

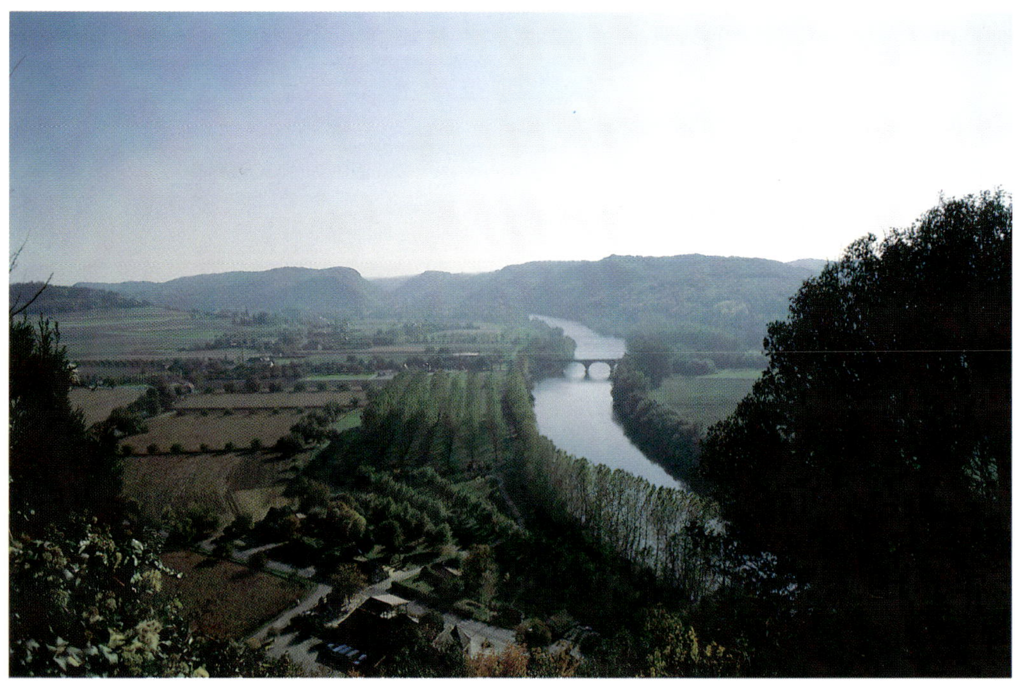

In landscapes, the sky may comprise a large portion of the shot. If you do not deliberately overexpose by a stop or two, the final shot will be underexposed, because the meter will take too much notice of it.

The main thing to remember is that meters are stupid. If you think the meter may be misjudging the scene, take control.

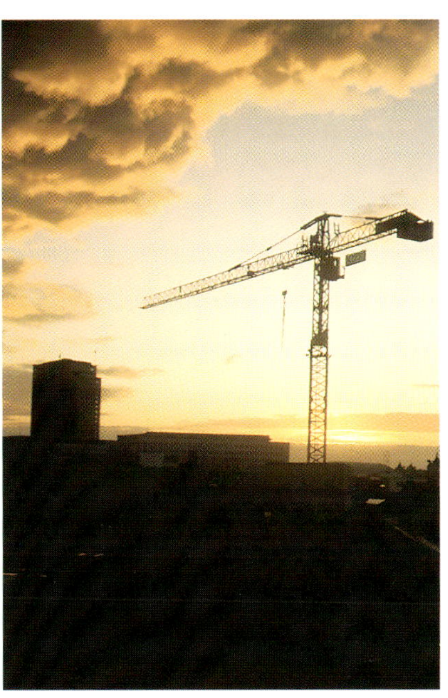

Above No exposure compensation was used in this shot: the result is a saturated colour in the sky but little detail in the rest of the shot.

Metering patterns Not all meters average the whole scene to determine the light level. There are five other types of in-camera metering: centre-weighted average, partial, spot, matrix/evaluative and off-the-film-plane. The last two are more complex, relatively recent systems on newer SLRs.

So that the photographer can tell if the meter reading is exposing correctly, the part of the scene that the camera is actually metering needs to be known.

Centre-weighted average metering disregards a section of the scene at the top of the frame, and is most influenced by light from the central portion of the frame, but still takes account of some light from outside that portion. As you move towards the edge of the frame, the light – irrespective of its brightness – influences the meter less and less. So, for example, light at the edge of the frame might be 10 stops (or exposure values – EVs) brighter than the central portion, but would influence the overall reading by one stop or less.

Partial metering uses only a part of the scene to read from, again in the centre. Any light coming from outside the reference circle in the viewfinder can be disregarded as it will not affect the meter.

Spotmetering is an extension of this. Using an even smaller part of the frame (2.5 per cent), the spotmeter takes its reading from the very centre. This is of limited value unless the subject at that

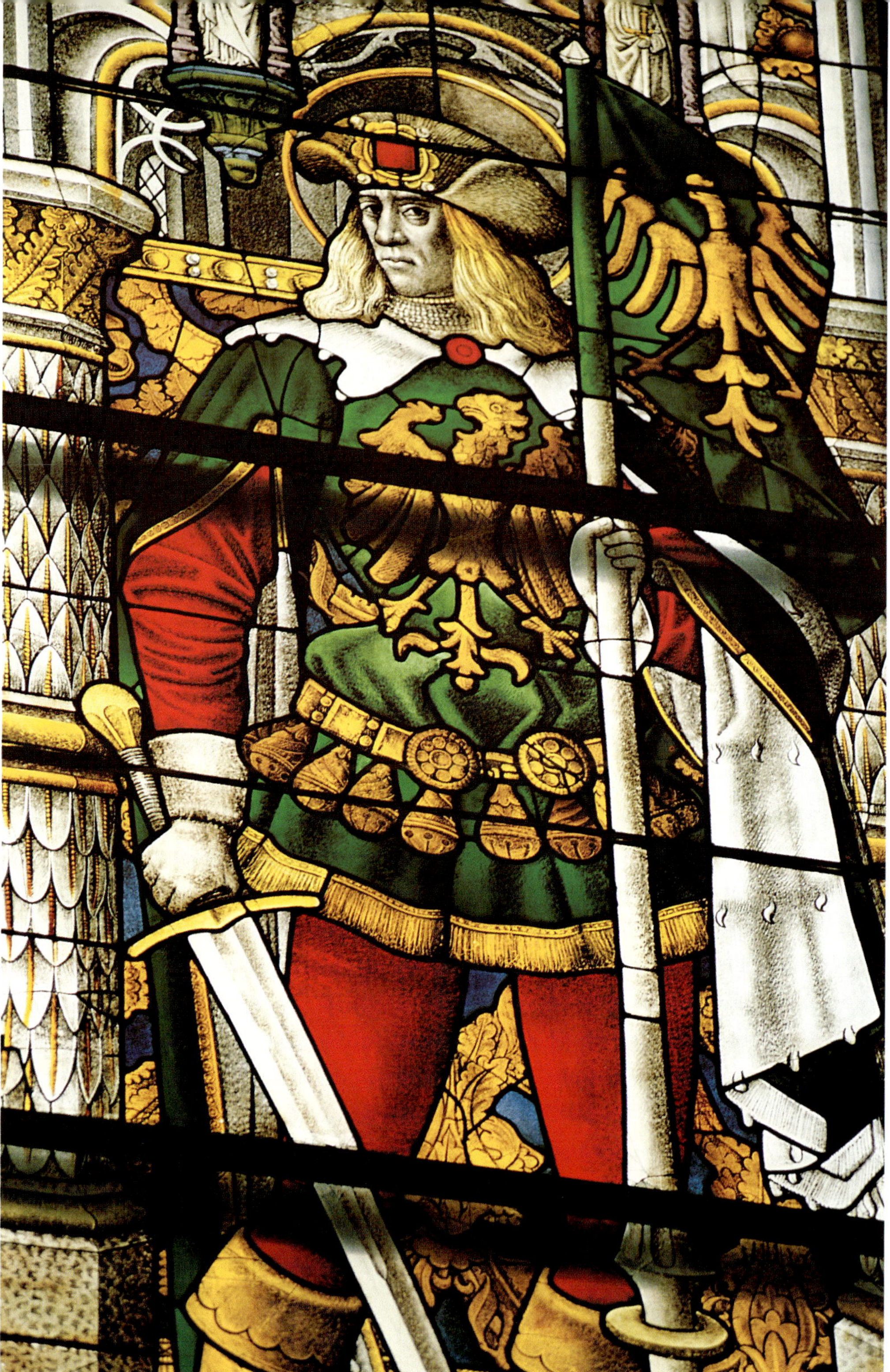

Metering

point is a mid-tone grey; but there is nothing to stop you, after composing the shot, from metering from another part of the scene. More selective meters like spot and partial allow you to do this without changing position, only requiring a slight alteration in the direction of the camera.

Matrix/evaluative uses a matrix of meter cells, and a computer in the camera then decides which cell(s) to use to calculate the exposure for the main subject, disregarding the brightest reading – most likely the sky – for example, and averaging the others. While matrix systems tend to be more accurate than centre-weighted average meters, their disadvantage is that the user does not know which part of the scene the meter is reading from.

Off-the-film-plane metering measures the light actually exposing the film by means of a cell pointing backwards towards the film. The system is most often used with flash to calculate when to switch off the flash during exposure.

Left Stained-glass windows are notoriously difficult to meter from, so it is worth taking a number of shots to see which one works best.

Below Bright light not only causes flare but also reduces contrast within the frame.

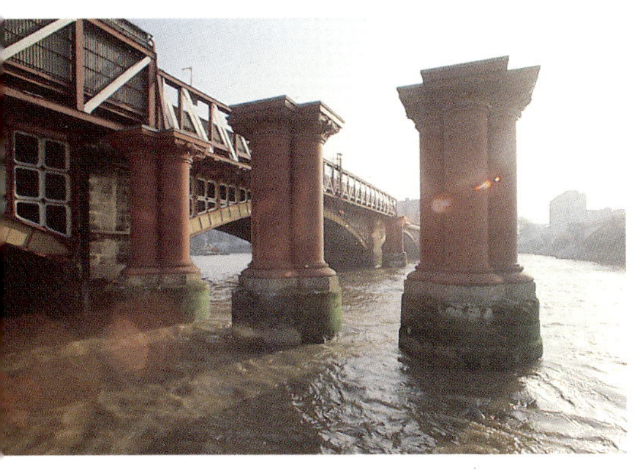

Bracketing Some scenes will be too complex in their combination of light and dark for you to be able to take control with confidence. In these cases, hedge your bets by shooting an extra exposure either side of your meter-inspired guess.

This 'bracketing' of the probable exposure should yield at least one 'correctly' exposed shot of a scene that is difficult to judge. The other reason for bracketing is that the correct exposure may not aesthetically be the best. If you slightly underexpose (by one third to half a stop) on slide film, colours become deeper and brighter. Slightly overexposing a shot with deep shadows means some of the detail within those shadows will be retained. The slight change in exposure that you get with bracketing can really make a picture.

Focusing and Depth of Field

Facing page, left to right The diagrams and corresponding pictures show what happens when the lens is focused correctly, focused in front of the subject (front focus), and focused behind the subject (back focus).

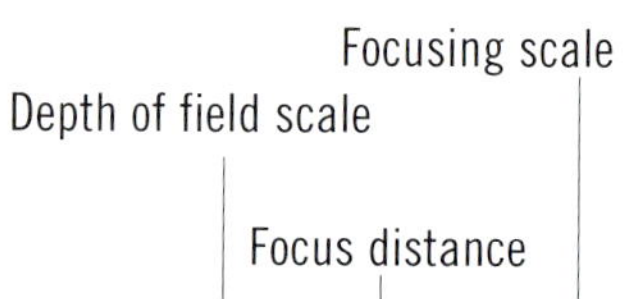

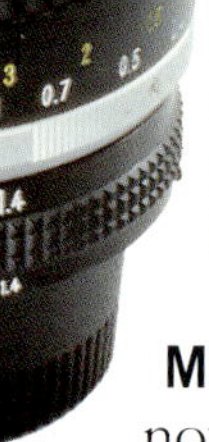

Light falling on a subject is reflected in all directions – otherwise we would be able to see the subject from only one position.

From each point on a subject within the field of view of the lens, it is only that light which hits the front of the lens that influences what is recorded on the film. From each point on the subject there is a 'solid' cone of light with its apex at the subject and its circular base falling at the front element of the lens.

The job of the lens is to reverse this, forming a cone with its base at the front element of the lens and its apex at the film plane. When this apex is exactly at the film plane, the point on the subject is in focus.

If the apex is formed in front of or behind the film, the point on the subject will appear as a disc – an out-of-focus blob – on the film. Obviously there is a diameter of disc which cannot be distinguished from a point – depending on the viewing distance. This point is known as the circle of confusion.

If the lens is focused on a point at one distance, it will not be precisely found for a point at a greater or lesser distance. But if the disc formed on the film is the same size or smaller than the circle of confusion, it will still be sharp. The distance between the nearest and the furthest points that are acceptably sharp is known as the depth of field.

Manual Focusing Focusing a camera manually is not difficult, and is made easier by focusing aids

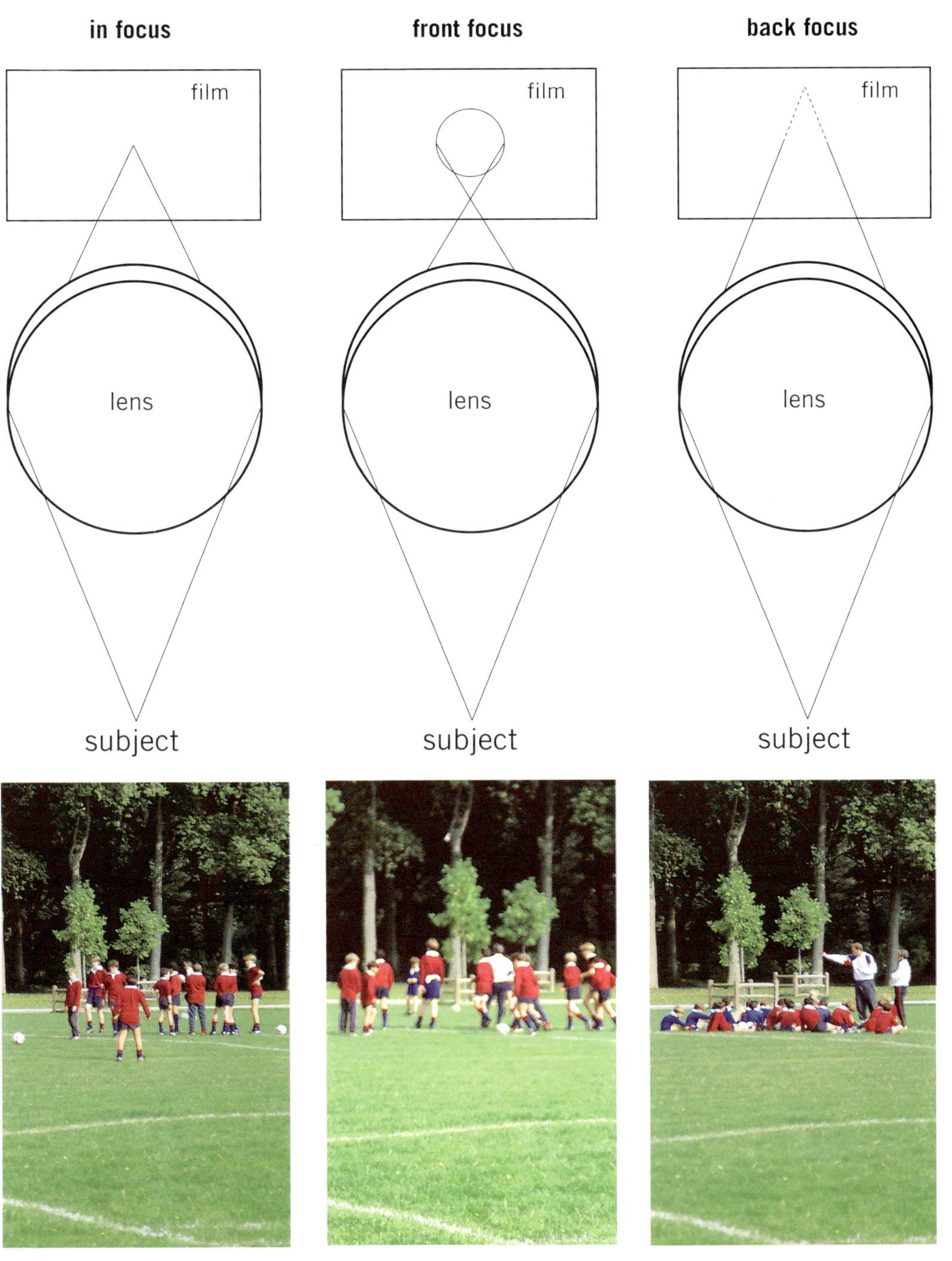
in focus
front focus
back focus
film
film
film
lens
lens
lens
subject
subject
subject

in the viewfinder. The first of these is the split-prism. When the subject is not in focus, the images in the two semi-circular prisms are away from one another. As the lens is gradually moved towards focus, the images move together until they form a seamless circle at the centre of the frame. The split of the prism may be either diagonal or horizontal.

Outside the split screen there is a microprism collar. This follows the same principle as the split-prism, but rather than showing a part of the image, the microprism collar either shimmers when out of focus, or is clear when in focus.

The rest of the viewfinder's focusing screen is made up of a sheet of ground or etched glass which has just enough texture for the image to form on it, but is transparent enough to allow a bright image to pass through it to the eyepiece of the viewfinder.

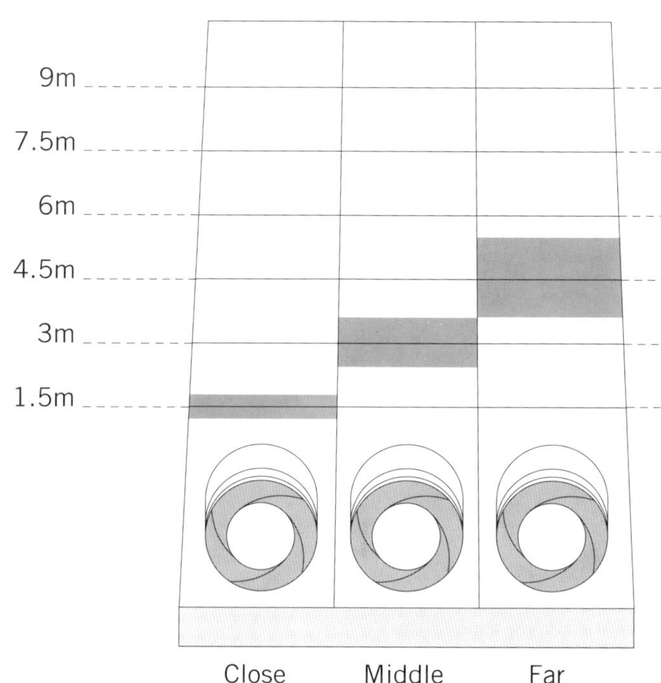

36 **Right** These three diagrams show the change of depth of field with subject distance, aperture and focal length.

Depth of field Three factors affect depth of field: subject distance, aperture and focal length.

Subject distance If you look at the focusing scale of an SLR's lens, it is apparent that the scale is not linear; the distances shown do not increase in a uniform way. The depth of field scale, on the other hand, is a linear scale, which is why photographers recommend focusing a third of the way into your desired depth of field.

Looking at the lens above, the focus is set for 0.9m. We can see from the scale that, at f/11, the nearest point in focus is 0.7m and the furthest point 1.3m – a depth of field of 60cm, with the focused point a third of the way in.

As you can see from the scale, the further away the subject the more depth of field there is for any given aperture. And by extension, the nearer the subject the less depth of field.

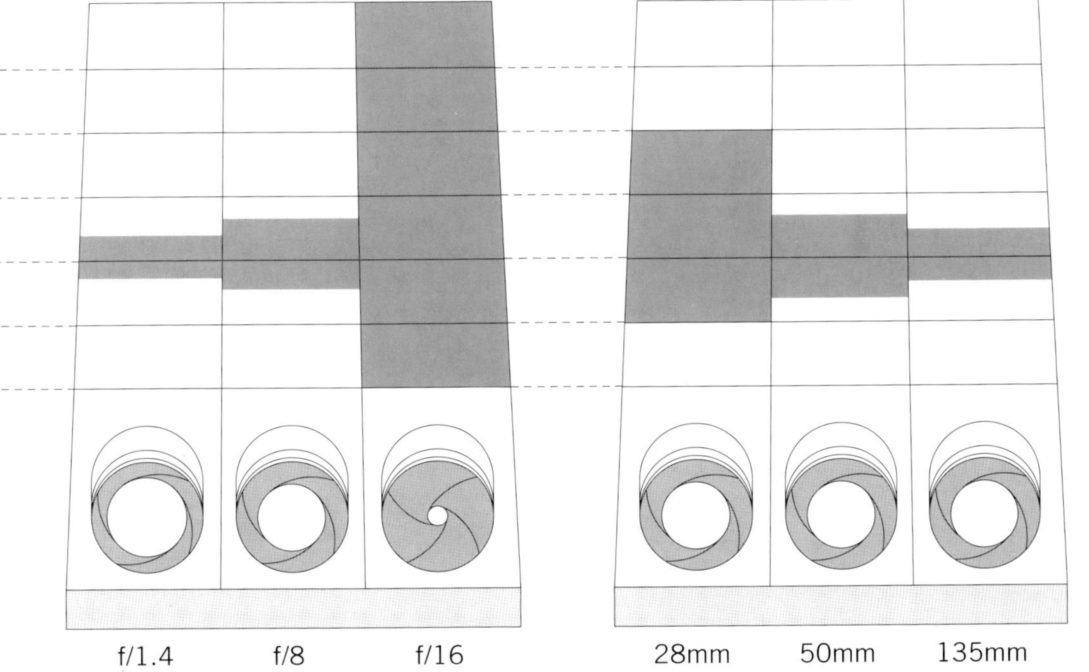

Aperture The smaller the aperture selected when shooting a scene, the smaller will be the base of the cone of light coming from the subject, and the more likely it is that out-of-focus discs will be smaller than the circle of confusion on the film – that is to say, they will be acceptably sharp. The wider the aperture the sharper the discs, and therefore more care must be taken with focusing as there is less depth of field.

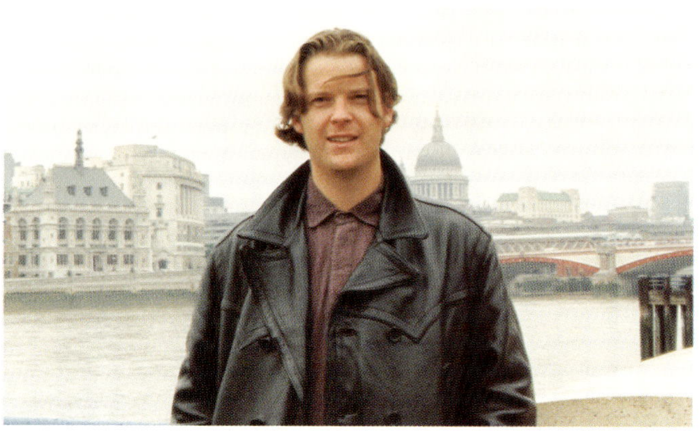

Above and facing page In the two pictures on the opposite page, there is no adequate depth of field to record both the portrait subject and the background in sharp focus at the same time. By using a lens with a shorter focal length, a smaller aperture and focusing between the two subjects, both are sharply recorded (above).

Focal length The key to the effect of focal length on depth of field is image magnification. If a subject is massively blown up by a telephoto lens, out-of-focus blobs will appear quite large. If a subject is much reduced, points on the subject are so small that it is impossible to tell the out-of-focus discs from in-focus points.

From the above three criteria, it is relatively simple to calculate that for maximum depth of field you should use a wideangle lens set to its minimum aperture with the subject a long way away. Conversely, to get the minimum possible depth of field, you need a long telephoto lens set to its widest aperture with a close subject.

Depth of field preview If your camera has a depth of field preview, you can see what will actally come out in focus in your photograph. SLR camerass view a scene with the lens set to maximum aperture – so as to give the brightest possible image in the viewfinder – so it is not possible to see what will be in focus when the picture is taken. However, the depth of field preview closes the lens down to the set aperture to allow viewing of what is in focus to be accurate. When the preview is pressed the screen darkens and the full extent of the depth of field is visible.

The drawback is that there is less light getting through to the viewing screen, and unless the scene is bright it can be difficult to see anything at all, let alone what is in focus. But this loss of light is partially compensated for by the expansion of the pupil of the eye.

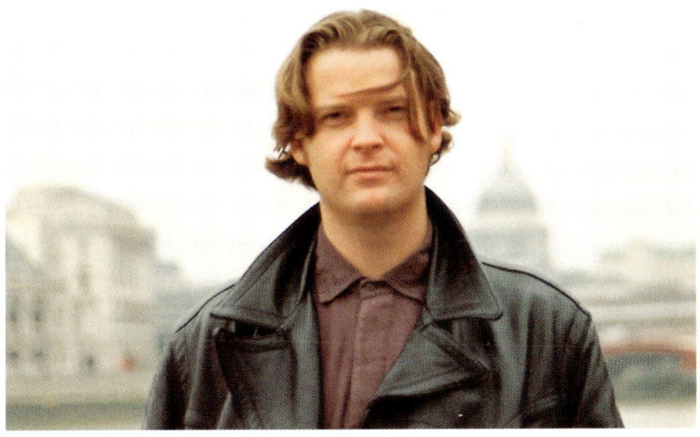

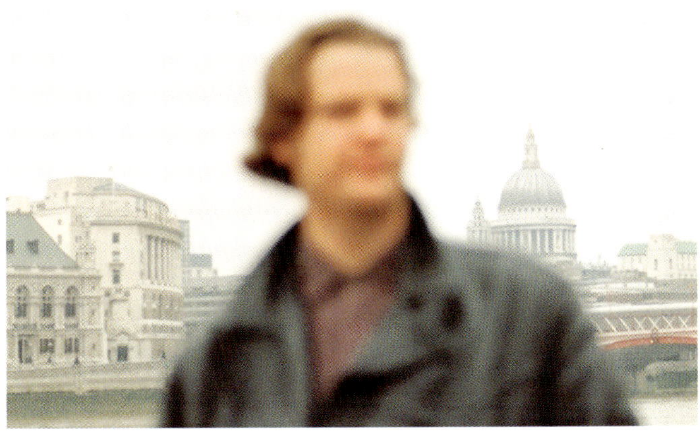

Hyperfocal distance If you are dealing with a subject at some distance away – effectively at infinity – and you want to maximize the depth of field, do not focus at infinity as this means you will be wasting a great deal of depth of field.

To maximize depth of field, set the aperture to its minimum setting (around f/16), focus the lens at infinity, and see what the depth of field scale (engraved on the lens) indicates is the nearest point of sharp focus. This point is known as the hyperfocal distance. Now set the lens to be focused at this distance, and objects at infinity will still be in focus, but you will also have gained extra foreground depth of field, ending at half the hyperfocal distance.

Autofocus

Some people curse it, others could not shoot pictures without it. Is autofocus (AF) the best invention since sliced bread or merely another irritating way that cameras take control away from the user?

The answer is – both. Autofocus is only a problem when the camera user does not know when it will fail and why. With this knowledge, it is relatively easy to bend the camera to your own will.

There are two main types of AF system: passive and active. The passive system tends to be used mainly on SLRs, while active systems are used on compact cameras.

SLR autofocus Passive autofocus (otherwise known as TTL – through-the-lens – phase detection or contrast detection) is based on a very simple principle, namely that a focused subject will exhibit higher contrast than an unfocused subject. You can easily test this by focusing (manually) your camera on a brightly lit sheet of newspaper text positioned at the minimum focusing distance of your camera lens. When the image is sharply

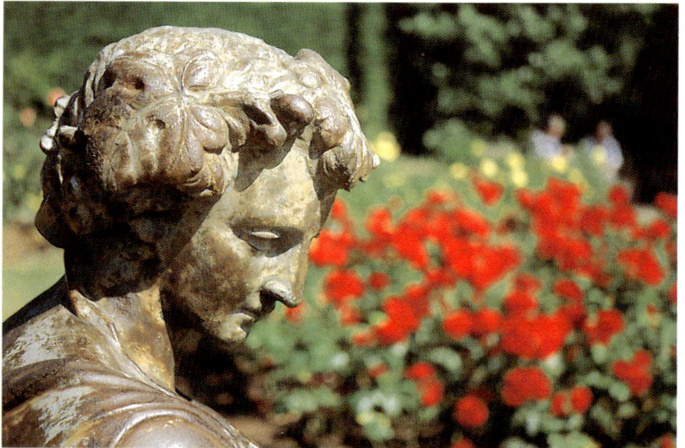

Right When holding an AF SLR for a vertical shot for a subject with vertical lines, establish the focus with the camera horizontal and then recompose the shot.
Left Three-beam AF systems will tend to focus on the nearest subject.

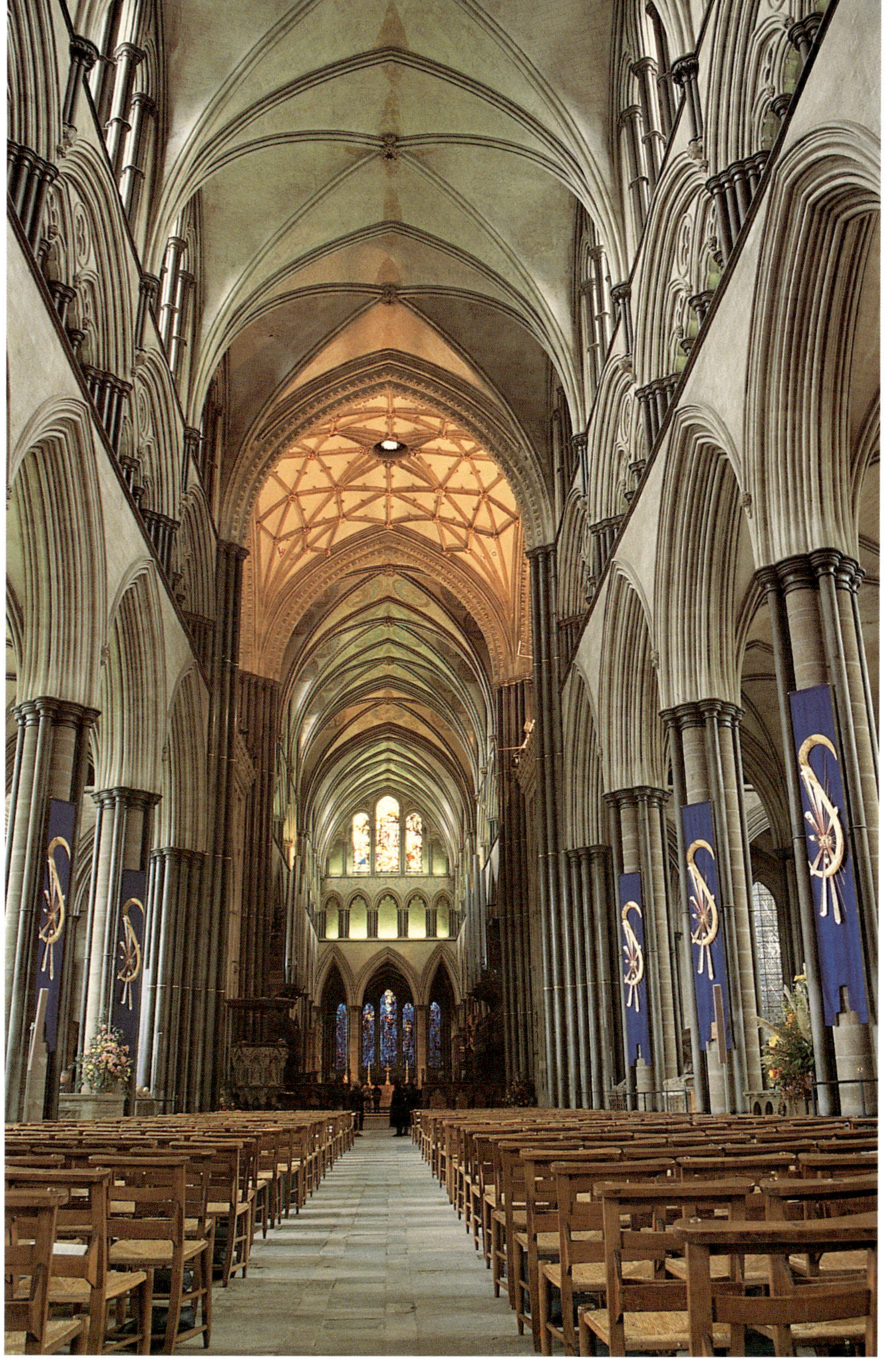

in focus, the contrast between the black type and white paper is massive. Refocus the lens at infinity without changing the newspaper-to-camera distance, and all you can see is grey blocks where the text columns are. Turning the principle around, you have the basis for a focusing system: that an image is in focus when the contrast is at its maximum.

The way cameras detect this contrast is by using an array of CCDs (charge coupled diodes) which convert the amount of light falling on them into electronic signals that are interpreted by the camera. By automatically focusing the lens forwards and backwards, the camera is able to establish at which focus position there is most contrast, and the lens is left at that position.

Effectively, these CCD arrays are a long line of individual light-sensitive cells. Generally the line is horizontal, and the camera is therefore able to detect subjects with vertical lines. Some, more sophisticated (and expensive) SLRs have sensors that can detect horizontal lines (with vertical sensors) as well as vertical lines; others have their double arrays (two rows of 100 cells) tilted at a slight angle so that subjects with horizontal lines will be less likely to fool the AF system. Light from the subject reaches the CCDs by a semi-silvered part of the main mirror, which allows a portion of the light to pass through it. This is then reflected down through a lens and focused onto the CCD array.

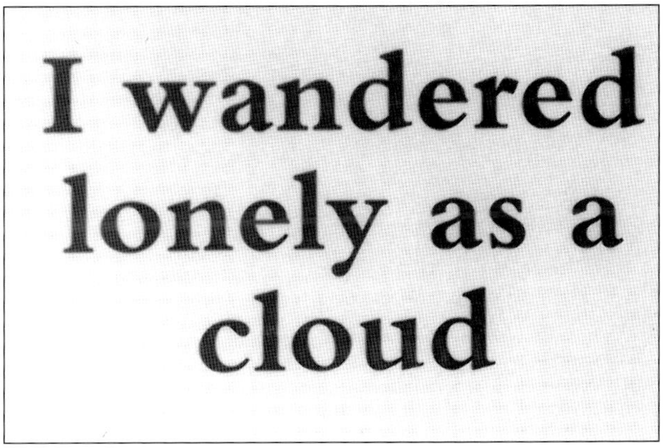

Below and right SLR autofocus systems work on a contrast detection basis. When the lens is in focus (below), the maximum contrast between light and dark is achieved. When the lens is nearly focused (top right), there is fringing between light and dark. When the lens is out of focus (bottom right), black and white subjects merge to form a woolly grey image.

When passive AF fails Given that the passive AF system is based on the ability of the CCD arrays to

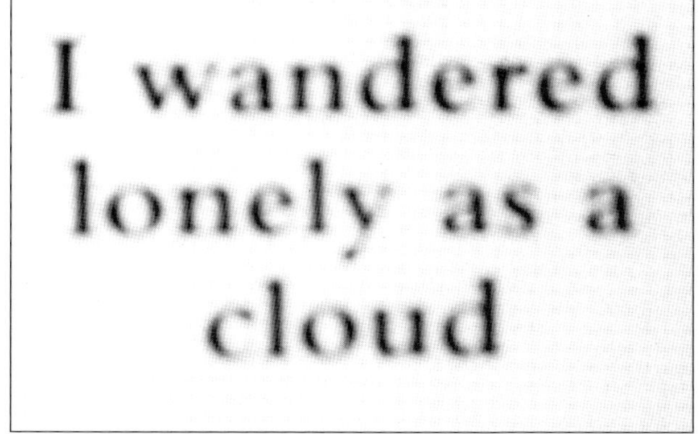

detect contrast, there are some circumstances when they will not work unassisted. For instance, if you have a scene where there is virtually no contrast, or where the subject and background have practically the same tone, the AF system will have problems establishing a focus. The solutions to this are either to find a point at an equal distance from the camera where there is some contrast for the AF system to detect, or focus manually and close down the aperture a stop to give more depth of field.

However, lack of contrast is not always a result of too diffuse a light source. If a scene is very dark or even pitch black, there will obviously be very little contrast between the subject and background. Similarly if there is very bright light, the autofocus system will be unable to cope adequately. The solutions are as before.

As the contrast detection system is made up of a line of sensors, it is also possible that you might have problems where the subject is a repeating pattern which coincides in its frequency with the CCD array. For example, the bricks of a large building might be placed so that each brick lands exactly on a CCD sensor. There will be no difference between the readings obtained by the individual cells, so the camera will be unable to focus. To overcome this problem (and, similarly, when the camera cannot focus on a horizontal line), simply turn the camera through to the upright position or through 45° and the CCD array should have something to bite on.

In order to overcome problems of lack of light or contrast, some cameras have a built-in pattern emitter that the AF system can focus on when it reflects off the subject. Although these work well in practice for near subjects (up to about 5–8 metres), they are no use for distant or very bright subjects, and they are also a dead giveaway that you are about to take a picture, as they work by projecting a bright red light at the subject.

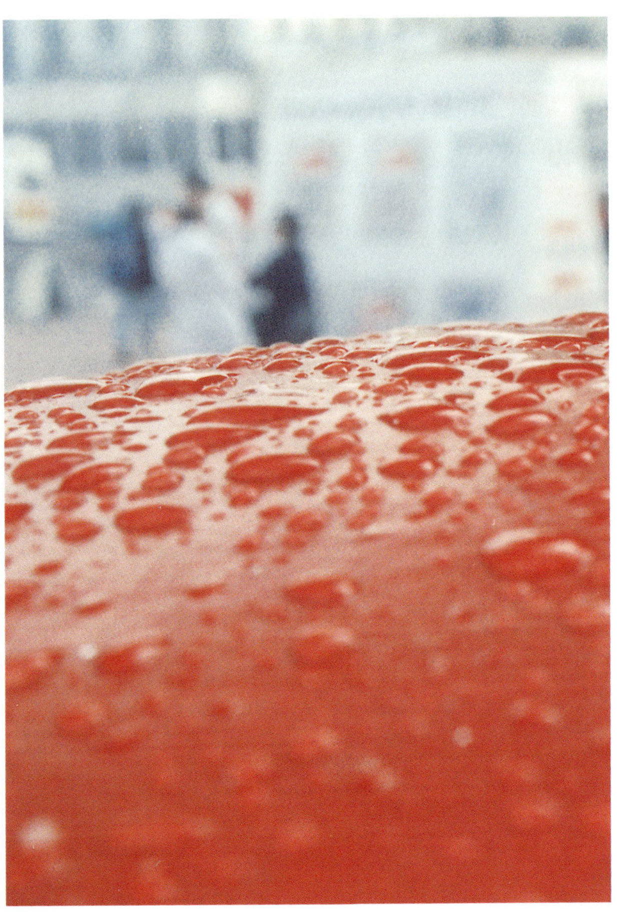

Above When shooting with an AF camera, bear in mind that it will only focus on what you point it at. In this case, the camera has focused on the red surface on which it was placed to steady it.

General AF problems After establishing that AF systems do not always focus correctly, there is another point. AF systems, like all computers, are stupid. They will focus only on the point at which they are aimed. If your subject is not along the axis the camera is aimed at, chances are it will not be focused correctly.

The classic error of focusing is to point a camera at a pair of subjects, although the focus frame lies in between them. The camera duly focuses on the background, giving a crisp shot of a tree with two blurred people in front of it.

The way to overcome this is to use the focus lock. Most AF cameras have a focus lock so you

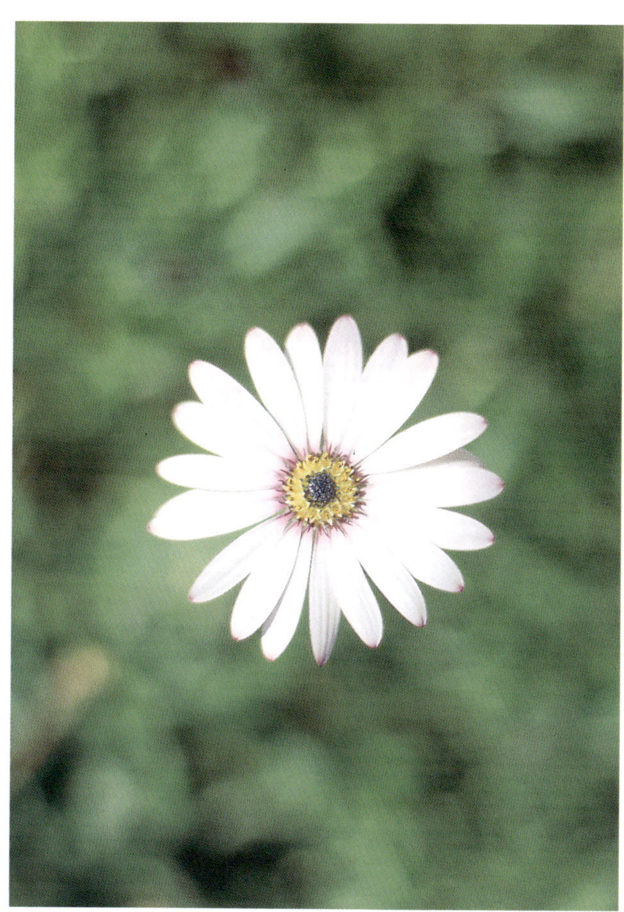

Above Press the shutter release halfway to lock the focus when the subject is dead centre. This has produced a sharp image of the main subject, the flower, while the background remains a blur.

can focus on the subject, hold that focus position and then recompose the shot in the knowledge that no matter how you now compose the scene, the main points of interest will remain sharp.

The other great problem with AF systems is moving subjects. In the time between the shutter release being pressed and the shutter actually opening and exposing the film, the subject will have carried on moving. Result: out of focus subject. Sophisticated AF SLRs have predictive focusing; that is, they calculate how far the subject will travel in the time between pressing the button and exposure, and focus the lens at that position for the moment of exposure. None of these systems is foolproof, and you still have to track the subject so that the focus frame is precisely at the centre of the subject – which removes some of the compositional freedom from the photographer.

The solution is, once again, to preset the focus – either manually or with a focus lock – at a specific point. Just before the subject gets to that point, trip the shutter. With a bit of luck, the image will be sharp. If the lighting levels allow (without selecting too slow a shutter speed), close down the aperture once again to get a little more depth of field.

Light

The word 'photograph' derives from two Greek words, *phos* and *graphos*, and literally translated means 'write light'. The importance of light in photography is self-evident; without light of some type, a photograph cannot be taken.

But there is a great deal more to photography than simply the presence or absence of light. The colour, quality, intensity and direction of light all affect not only the exposure but also the mood of a picture.

Artificial or natural light The amount of natural light falling on a scene cannot be controlled. If there is not enough for a desirable exposure then it needs to be supplemented or effectively

Right The clock tower is bathed in the subtle warm light of dusk.

Below The flame is recorded in this photograph as the harsh sunlight casts a shadow over it.

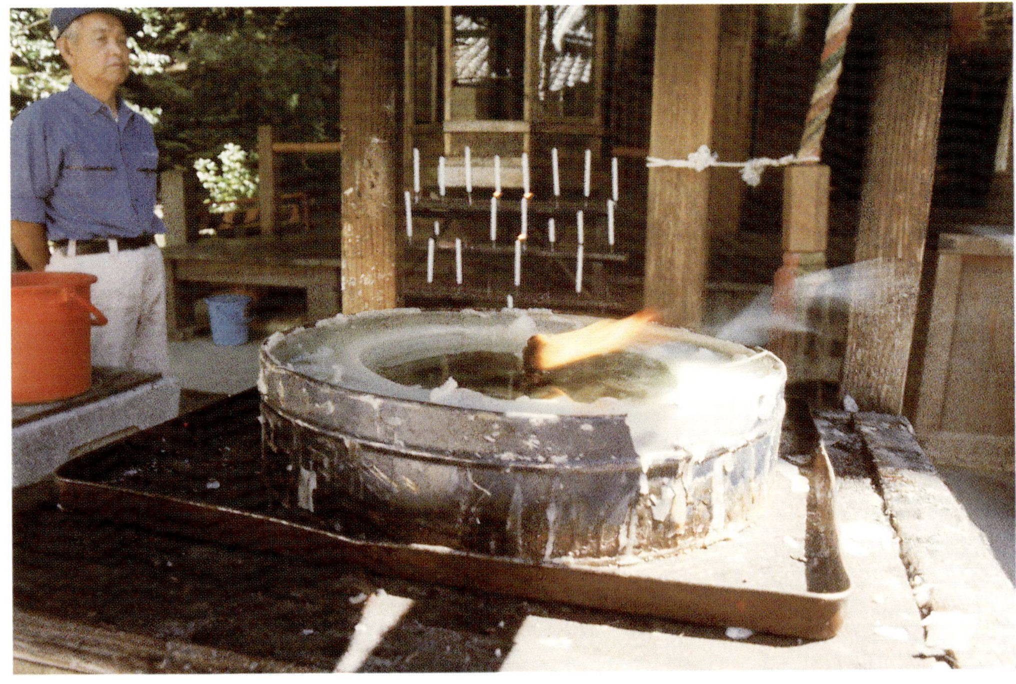

replaced by artificial illumination of one sort or another. Artificial light tends, by its nature, to be very directional, whereas natural light (other than direct sunlight) tends to be even and virtually shadowless in its illumination. Artificial light has the advantage of being a great deal more controllable, and it can be more easily diffused, but it is more difficult to use for distant subjects, or for large areas.

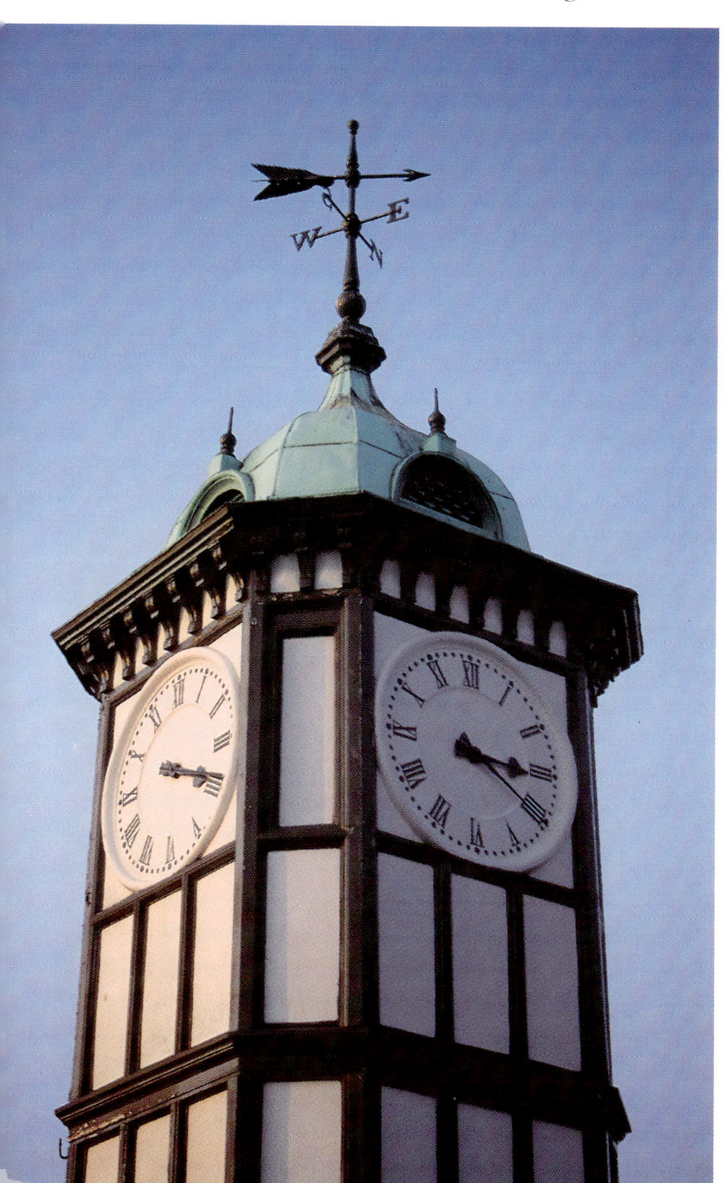

If using colour film, there is another consideration to be taken into account – the colour of the light. This is different for different types of light source.

Reciprocity failure and colour shift As we saw earlier with the reciprocity law (see page 19), opening up the aperture one stop (say, from f/8 to f/5.6) and using a shutter speed that is twice as fast (say, from 1/250sec to 1/500sec) will result in the same overall exposure. However, when shooting very long night exposures, this law no longer holds true. With very dark scenes the sensitivity of

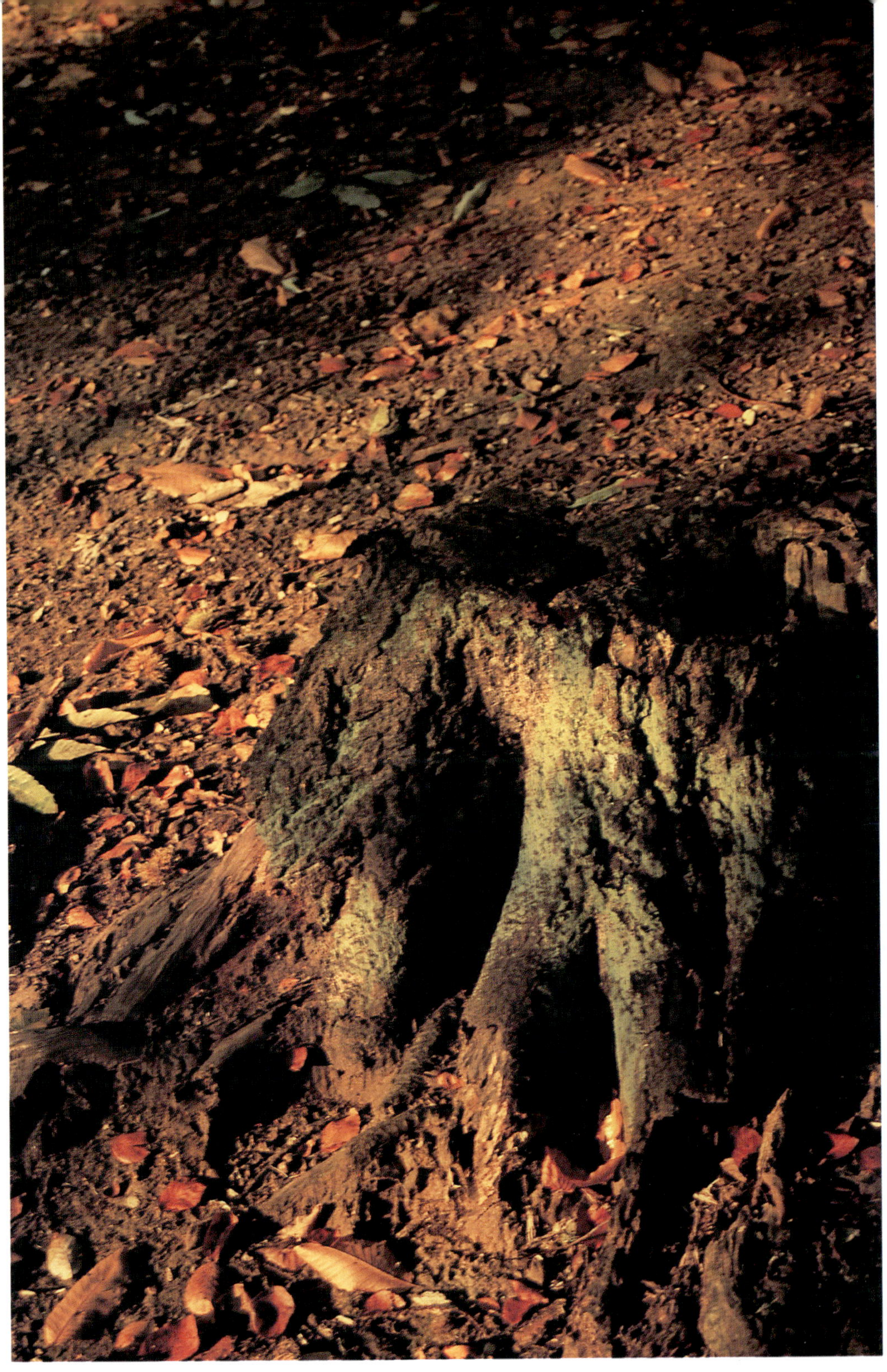

Light

Left Autumn leaves respond especially well to the glow of warm evening light.

the film decreases, and you have to give a longer exposure than the meter suggests to get a correctly exposed picture. Furthermore, the various colour layers in a film do not all lose their sensitivity at the same rate, so with very long exposures, there may be a colour shift in the picture.

Quality of light One of the most important factors in the mood of a shot is the scene's contrast. On days with very strong, undiffused sunlight, the contrast is likely to be high (that is, the number of stops difference between a meter reading taken from the brightest highlight and one taken from the deepest shadow is 10 or more). On an overcast or misty day, the difference between highlights and shadows is much less.

It is possible to get a combination of these two types of lighting on a day with low but broken cloud cover. Where the sun breaks through the clouds, you see majestic shafts of golden light breaking the otherwise grey illumination on the rest of the scene. Interior shots can also have this double illumination where the sun may directly light part of a room from one side, while diffused window light illuminates the rest from the other.

Time of year Because of the tilt of the earth and its annual orbit of the sun, the sun appears in the sky in different positions throughout the year. It also has varying strength depending on the time of year. In the summer, the sun is higher in the sky and will cast short but harsh shadows – especially difficult to deal with in external portraits. Because the sun is lower in the sky in winter, it casts long shadows, but its light has to pass through more atmosphere before reaching the surface, and this diffuses it more than summer light.

Time of day The nature and, especially, the colour of sunlight is as radically affected by time of day as by time of year. As light from the sun passes through the atmosphere, more and more ultraviolet and blue light is absorbed or scattered. As the sun goes down, the angle of its light means it passes through more atmosphere, leaving the redder end of the spectrum dominating the light.

White light It is natural to think of light being white, but white light does not really exist as a single entity. In fact, white light is simply a combination of all the colours of the visible spectrum. At the extremes of the spectrum are infrared (IR) and ultraviolet (UV) radiation. UV (and the bluer end of the visible spectrum) has a short wavelength and is least capable of penetrating environmental atmosphere and pollution. Thus it is only on a clear day with the sun high in the sky – and so having less atmosphere to penetrate – that the sky appears blue.

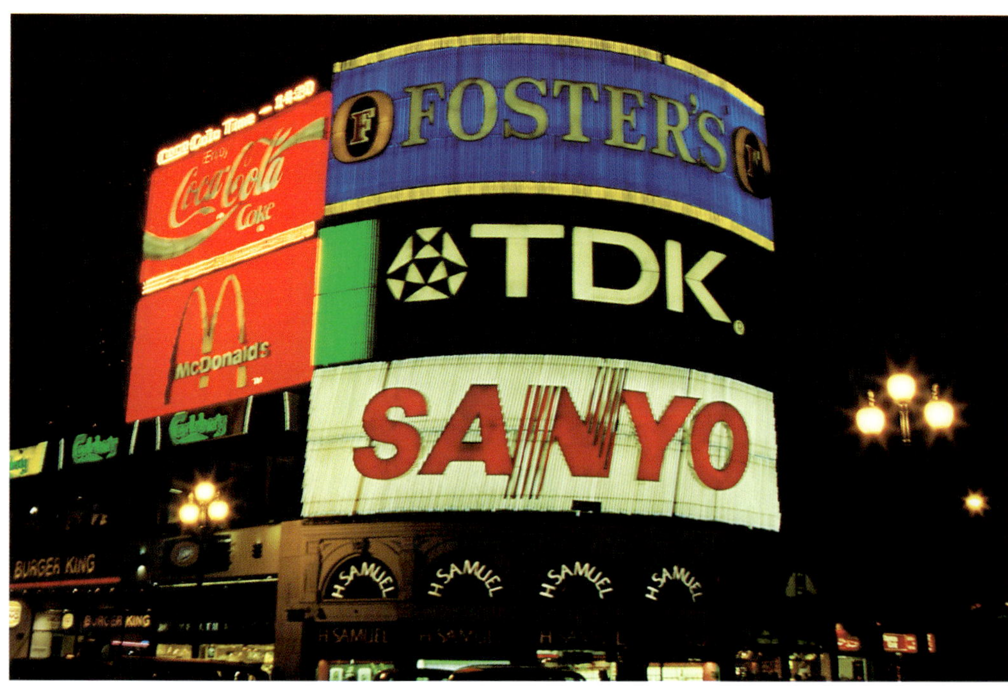

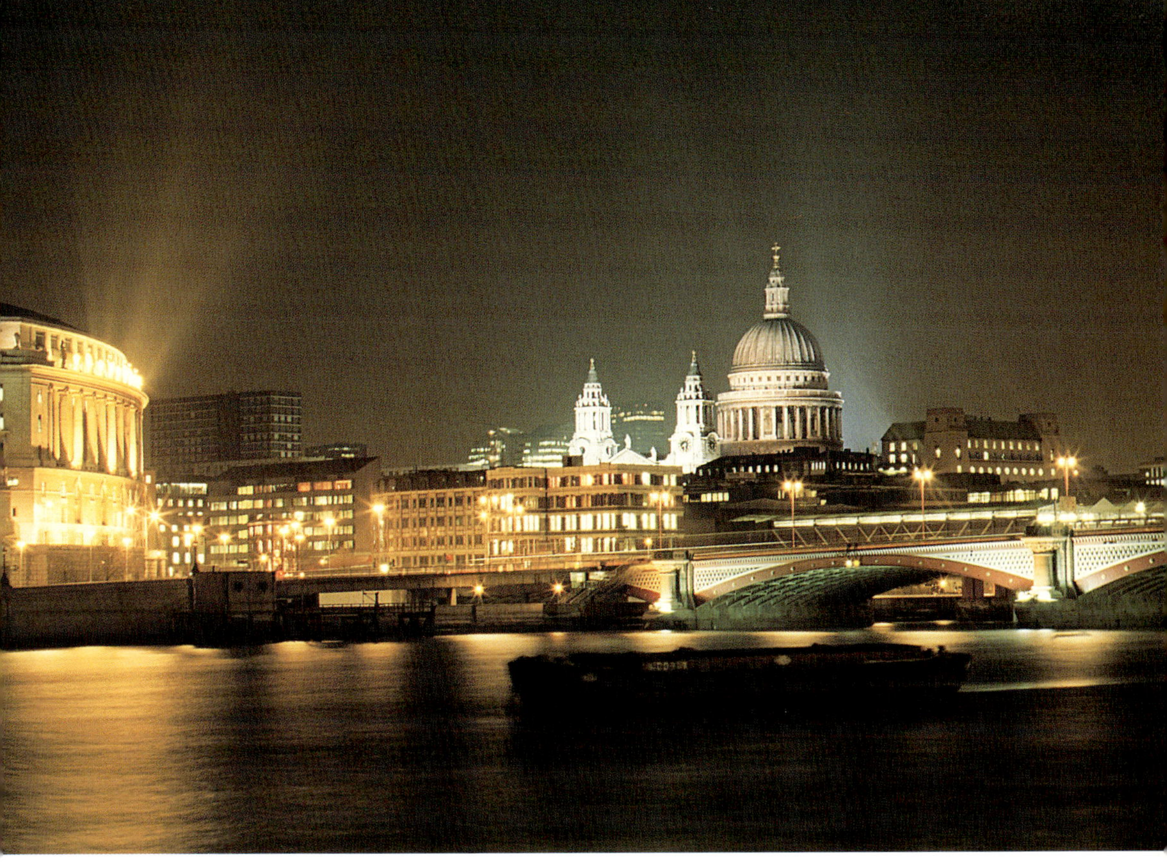

Above and left The human eye compensates for artificial light sources, but film shows their true colours in comparison to daylight. Mix fluorescent, tungsten, neon and sodium lights for a vivid multicoloured effect.

Colour temperature If a dull black metal object is progressively heated to higher and higher temperatures it starts to turn red, then orange, yellow and eventually white. Assuming that the object had not yet melted, if it were heated further it would start emitting blue light. The temperature at which these different colours are emitted is measured in degrees Kelvin (degrees C +273). The lower the colour temperature, the redder the light. The higher the colour temperature, the bluer the light.

The colour temperature of skylight is actually higher than that of sunlight. If the direct rays of the sun are blocked by cloud, the colour temperature of the light falling on a scene at noon in summer will be between 8500°K and 9500°K. If the scene is under direct sunlight, the temperature is nearer 5000°K to 6000°K; if the sky is totally overcast, the colour temperature is between 6500°K and 7500°K. The sun when it sets has a colour temperature of about 4000°K.

Filters

The human brain in conjunction with the eyes does not always see the same things a camera will see. We have discussed the effects of perspective change with subject distance, and magnification with focal length, but there are other ways in which this is true.

Although many photographers strive to achieve the most faithful reproduction of a scene, there is another approach to picture-taking – capturing the mood of a place. This is where filters can be useful. Most of them, as the name suggests, filter off part of the light coming into the lens, but others simply alter the way the light falls on the film. By using one or a combination of these factors, you can make a scene assume any mood you want.

Right Yellow filters perk up pictures by darkening skies while leaving clouds fluffy white.
Below The spectrum of colours that make up white light.

White light To understand how coloured filters work, think of white light as being composed of other colours. If you shine a red, a green and a blue light – the primary colours of light – so their beams overlap, the section where all three overlap is white.

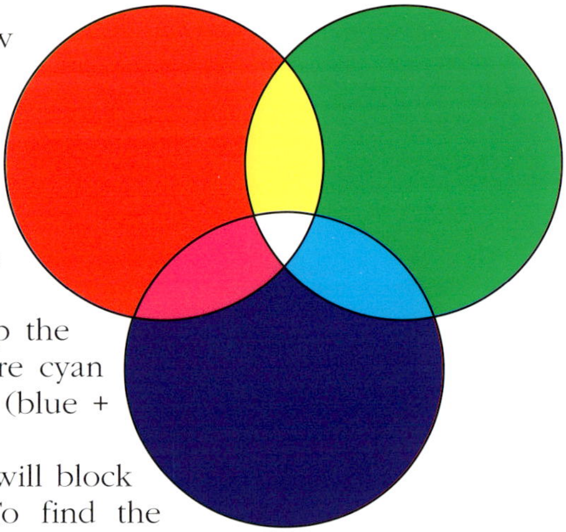

Where two primary colours overlap the result is a secondary colour. These are cyan (made up of blue + green), magenta (blue + red), and yellow (red + green).

When you put a filter on a lens it will block light of a complementary colour. To find the complement of a colour (say, red), draw a line from the centre of the red circle through the white section of the diagram, and it passes through the cyan section – thus the complement of red is cyan. The complement of green is magenta and of blue is yellow.

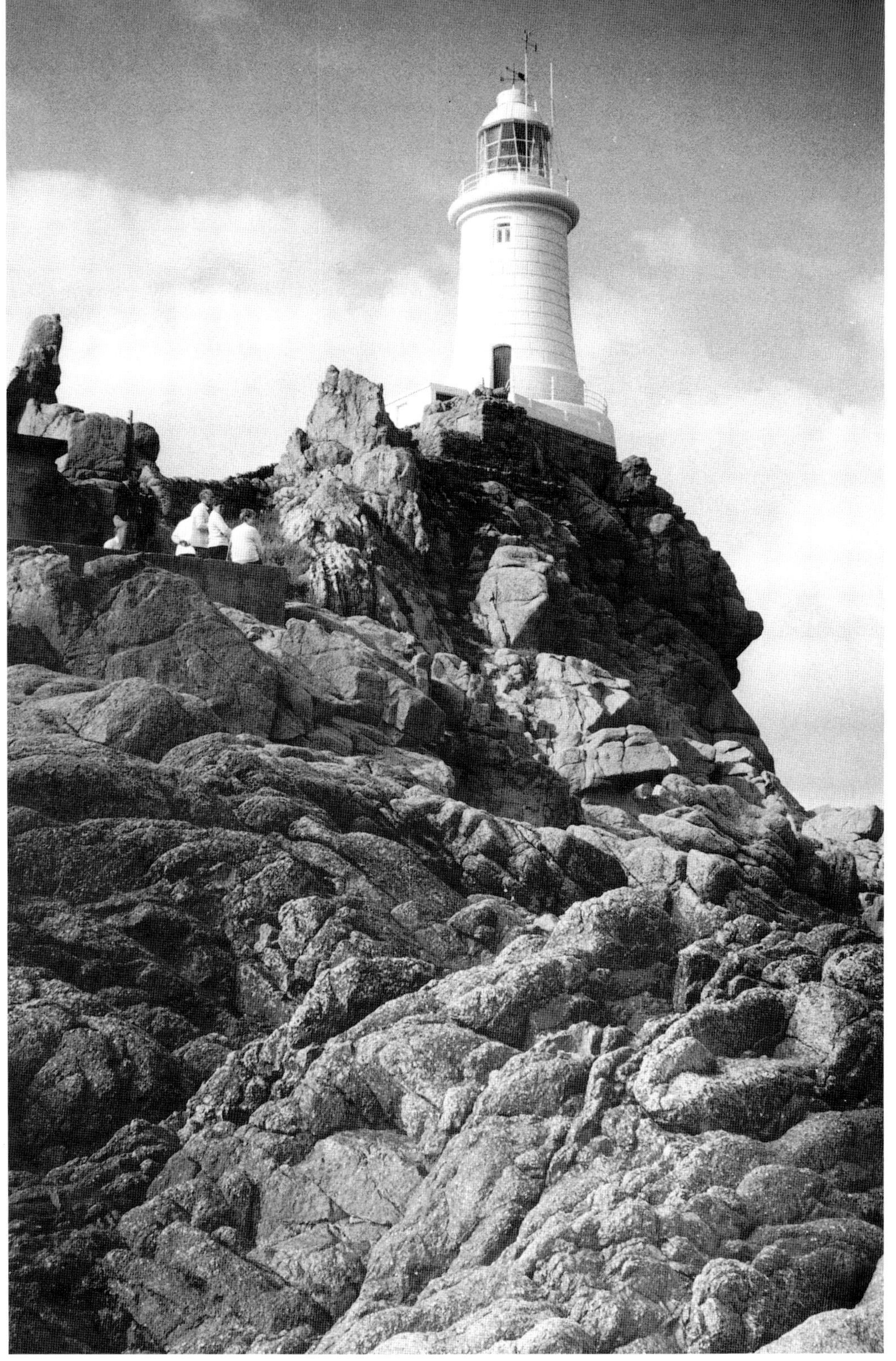

Filters with black and white film Putting coloured filters on a camera when it is loaded with black and white film may seem strange, but knowing that coloured filters remove their complement's colours from a scene allows great manipulation of tones in a scene. For example, yellow is the complement of blue, so putting a yellow filter on the lens when shooting in black and white will prevent blue light from the sky from making an impression on the film and darkening the sky.

When shooting with colour film, placing a filter of a particular colour over the lens will result in the final picture having that hue, and the complementary colours appearing much darker.

Density and exposure Remember that coloured filters are generally only dilute versions of the colour: although they will reduce the amount of light of a complementary colour from hitting the film, they will not completely prevent it all from hitting the film, or indeed from influencing the exposure meter.

The amount of light a filter removes from that falling on the lens can be different depending on the brand of the filter. Some manufacturers give the exposure loss in terms of the amount of extra exposure required, while others give the density of the filter. A dense red filter might carry the legend x8, indicating that it needs eight times the amount of light (three stops extra exposure) to allow the same amount of light to hit the film as if no filter was used. With through-the-lens (TTL) metering, this should be carried out automatically as the meter is measuring the amount of light passing through the filter. With filters (such as graduates) where the light-absorbing potential across the filter is not

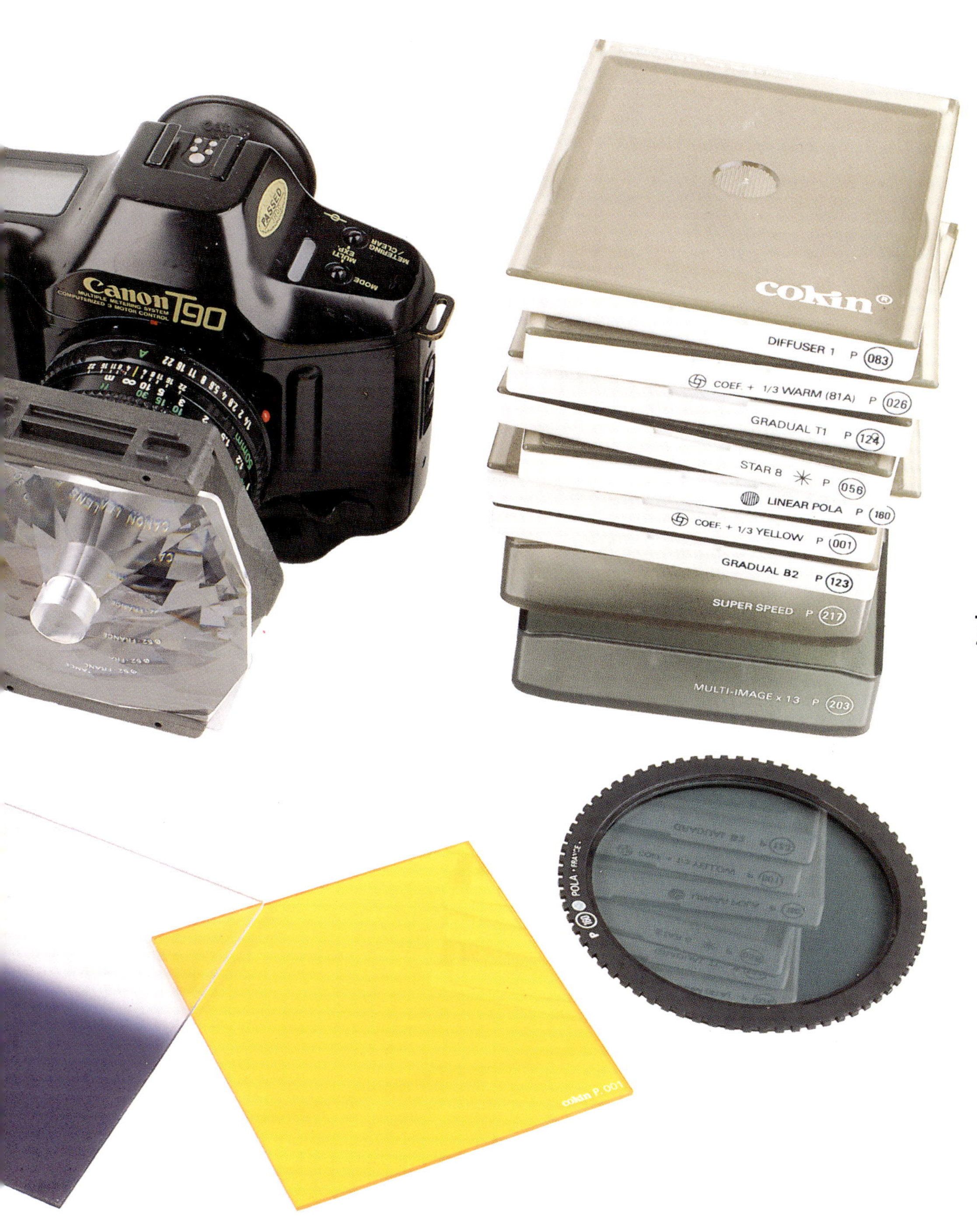
Canon T90
cokin
DIFFUSER 1 P 083
COEF. + 1/3 WARM (81A) P 026
GRADUAL T1 P 124
STAR 8 P 056
LINEAR POLA P 180
COEF. + 1/3 YELLOW P 001
GRADUAL B2 P 123
SUPER SPEED P 217
MULTI-IMAGE x 13 P 203
cokin P 001

equal, a little more thought is needed to make sure the exposure is spot-on.

Graduated filters Sometimes you do not want a filter that influences the whole of the scene. For example, if you want to change the appearance of the sky only, you will need a graduated filter. On this type of filter the upper half is a colour that decreases in density towards the middle, and the lower half is clear.

Despite their name, graduated filters can leave a clumsy 'join' mark where they change from clear to coloured if the aperture selected is too small. To prevent your picture from being obviously identifiable as a filter shot, shoot with a wide aperture so the two halves blend into one another seamlessly.

With tobacco- or reddish-coloured graduates you can turn a bland sky into a sunset – even

Below Combining a yellow filter with an orange graduate gives this landscape a surrealistic look.

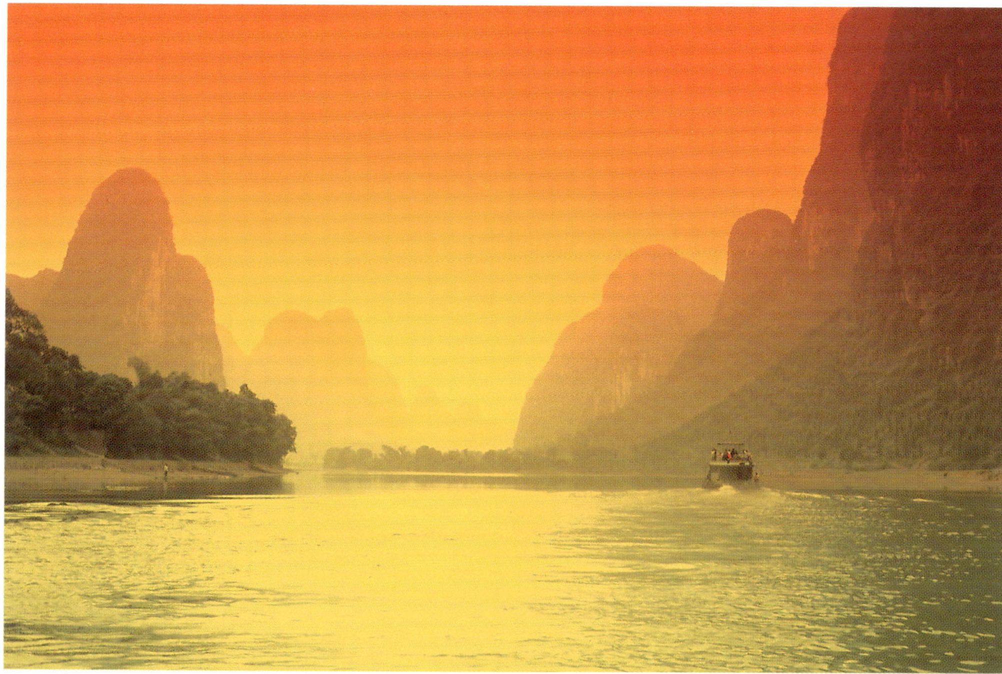

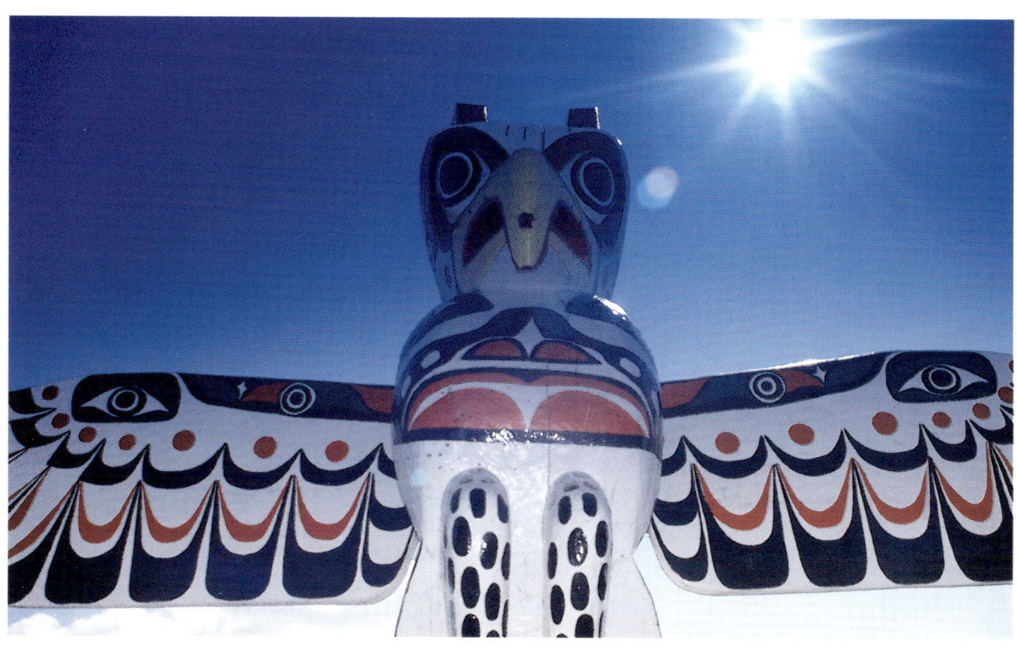

though it may have been taken at 10am. When the sky is much brighter than the landscape below it, grey graduates let you reduce the influence of the sky on the meter without altering the colour rendition. This means you can obtain not only a more balanced scene, but that there is also more chance of getting the exposure correct.

Above A blue graduate can spice up a flat sky. Normally shots including the sun in the frame have skies which are far less blue than when the sun is some distance out of the frame.

Polarizing filters

Light can be considered to travel as vibrations in different planes. When it bounces or reflects off anything non-metallic, it becomes polarized (it vibrates in only one plane), or partially polarized (it vibrates in a restricted number of planes). A polarizing filter simply repeats this effect by allowing only light vibrating in a similar plane to pass through it. Light polarized in completely different planes to the filter is not transmitted.

Polarizing filters can be rotated, so with an SLR it is possible to see when the filter is having its maximum effect on reflections (that is, polarized light) by turning the filter until they disappear. Skylight is partially polarized, so by rotating the filter it is possible to remove some of the light, to make the sky look darker and bluer. To maximize the polarizing effect on skies, try and point the camera at 90° to the sun's position in the sky. Point it at the sun, and the effect will be nil.

Special effects Some filters can be used to create a sense of the fantastic and surreal. Probably the most popular effects filter is the starburst (a clear filter with parallel lines at two or three different angles scratched on it), which gives any light source a bright star effect. The smaller the aperture used, the greater the effect will be.

Other special effects filters include the multi-prism, which gives a number of identical images on the same frame, and the superspeed, which gives a static object the impression of movement by blurring the back of it with a plastic prism.

Below A polarizing filter can drastically reduce the reflections coming off non-metallic surfaces such as glass or water. Shooting at 50–60° to these surfaces will give the maximum polarizing effect. When shooting face on to a reflecting surface, a polarizer will have no effect. It will also not affect mirror reflections.

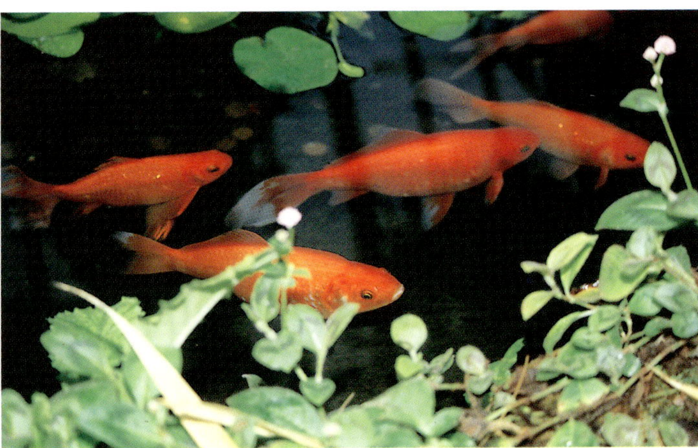

Other filters A large number of other filters are available in different formats (either screw-on or system), but the three main ones not mentioned so far are UV (which eliminates ultraviolet light and haze), skylight (which does the same but also warms up the scene a touch) and diffusion (which softens the look of a picture) – especially useful for portraits. Skylight and UV filters are also useful for protecting the lens against grit and moisture.

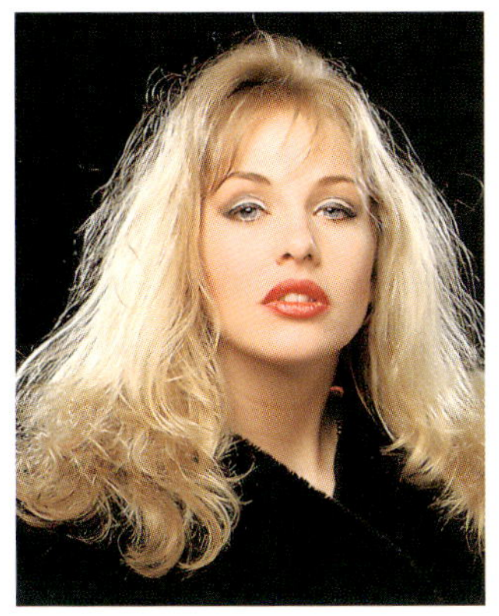

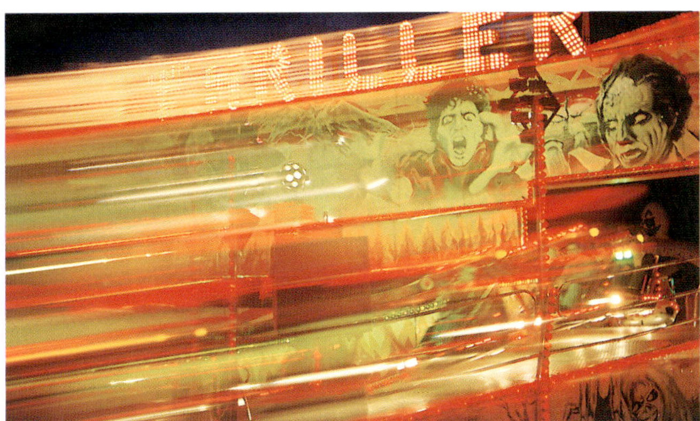

Above and below Diffusion filters make portraits look romantic by softening the highlights and removing fine skin blemishes and evening skin tones.
Right, top to bottom Special effects filters such as speed, multi-image and starburst can completely change the look of a scene – but try to use them sparingly.

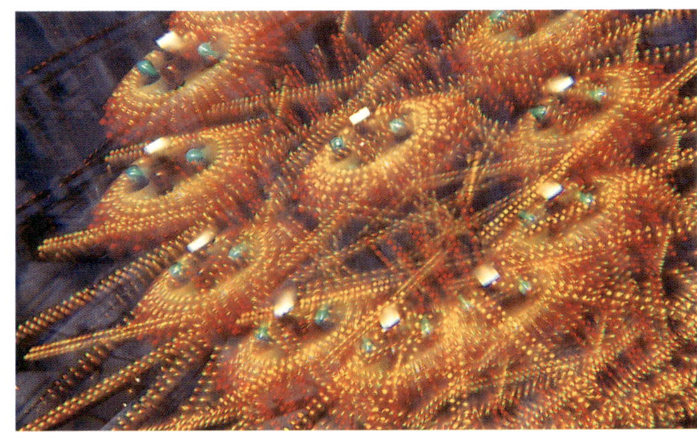

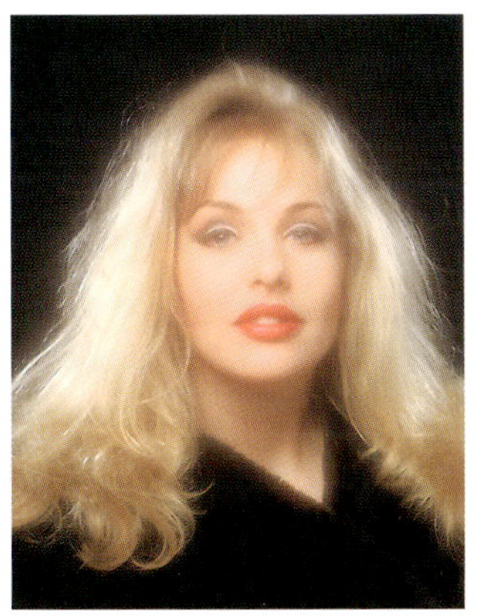

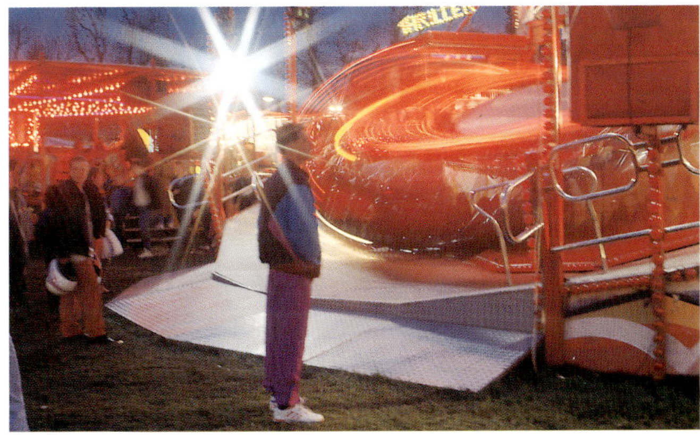

Flash

Imagine if you could place the sun at any position in the sky, alter its brilliance to your needs and take it indoors with you. Well, you can – almost.

Carrying a portable electronic flash unit with you is effectively the same as having your own personal sun; but without knowing how it works and when it does not, it can be every bit as capricious as the one in the sky.

The tube At the heart of every flash unit are two elements: a flash tube and a power source to fire it. The flash tube contains a mixture of gases, generally argon, xenon and krypton. Just before the main flash, a triggering voltage is applied to the outside of the tube which ionizes the gas mixture inside, thus temporarily altering it so that the gases can conduct electricity. The main pulse of electricity through the gases is in the form of an intense spark: the flash.

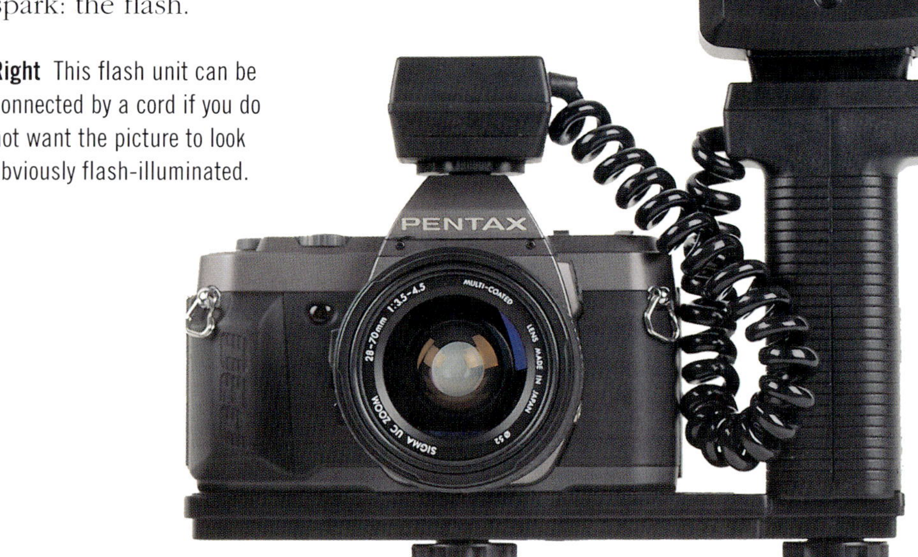

Right This flash unit can be connected by a cord if you do not want the picture to look obviously flash-illuminated.

Although firing a flashgun requires voltages of anywhere between 150V and 15,000V, most guns use either two or four batteries with a combined voltage of 3–6V. The whine you hear when a gun is charging up is the conversion of this 3V or 6V into high voltage alternating current (AC) before it is subsequently converted to high voltage direct current (DC) to fire the gun.

Inverse square law If you double the distance between a light source, such as flash, and an object, the object receives only a quarter of the light – not half, as you might expect. This effect is known as the inverse square law. With electronic flash, any change in subject-to-flash distance will affect the amount of illumination, meaning you have to alter either the exposure setting on the camera or the length of the flash burst.

Below If you select a shutter speed faster than the maximum flash synchronization, the frame will not be completely exposed.

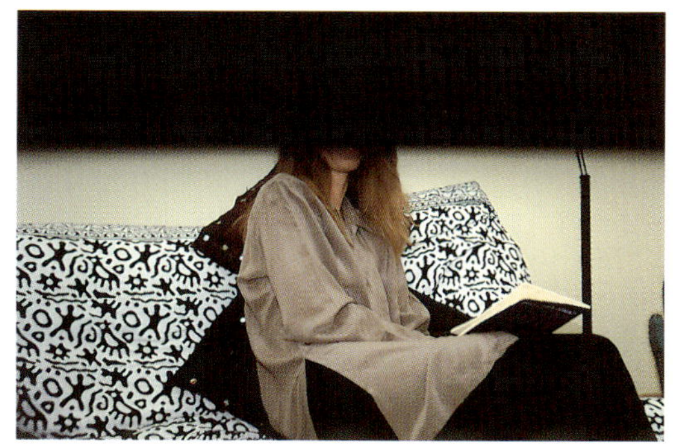

Camera and flash exposure The easiest way to understand the details of flash exposure calculation is to start by assuming you are in a pitch-black room. Most flashguns have a flash duration of between 1/1000sec and 1/125,000sec, and the fastest flash synchronization available on most cameras is 1/125sec, so the shutter speed chosen in our black room scenario is irrelevant. This is because the flash burst is always so much shorter than the shutter speed, and no other light apart from the flash is entering the lens. However, if a shutter speed faster than the maximum synchronization of the flash unit is selected, only a portion of the frame will be illuminated. Therefore, to alter the exposure to allow for different subject/flash distances, with a constant film speed, the aperture needs to be changed.

Guide numbers The easiest way to calculate the aperture required for a particular distance is to use the flashgun's guide number (GN). This is the f-number multiplied by flash-to-subject distance in metres (for use with ISO 100 film), and is given in your flashgun's manual. To find out the required aperture, divide subject distance by guide number.

For example, for a subject distance of 7.5m with a flash with a GN of 15, the required aperture is 15 ÷ 7.5 = 2, so the f-number is f/2. If the subject were 2.7m away, an aperture of f/5.6 (15 ÷ 2.7) would give the correct exposure. Charts showing the correct aperture for a certain subject distance and film speed are often given on the flashgun.

Automatic and through-the-lens flash Most current flashguns are automatic to some degree. The most common type is where the user sets the camera's lens to an aperture (governed only by the film speed in use) stated on the flashgun. The gun has a built-in light-sensitive cell, and when the flash is fired, this calculates when the subject has received enough light and turns off the flash. This removes the need to guess distance, as long as the subject lies within the range for the given film speed.

With through-the-lens flashmetering, you can set any aperture you desire for artistic effect. When the flash is fired, the camera's meter measures the light coming through the lens and stops the flash burst when the correct exposure is reached.

Between these two levels of operation is flash dedication: when the flash is fully charged, the camera automatically sets the maximum flash synchronization speed. Some cameras, when set to program mode, will also allow the flashgun to set the required aperture on the lens automatically.

Flash range The nearest and furthest points that can be illuminated correctly with flash are governed by the aperture range of the lens and the

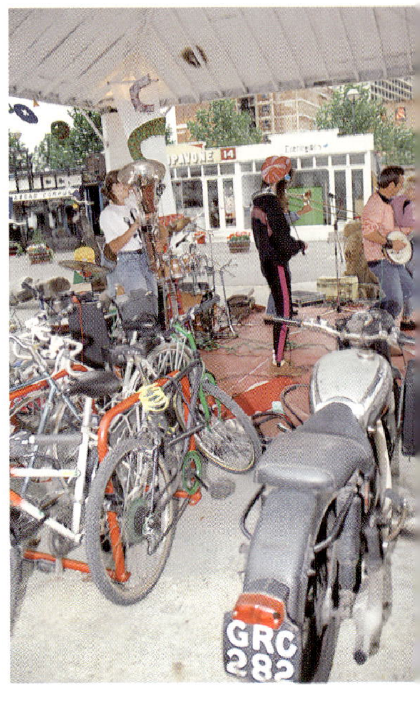

Above When used in shadowy covered areas, flash helps keep detail and allows use of a shutter speed fast enough radically to reduce camera shake.

speed of the film. Using ISO 400 film instead of ISO 100, you can shoot objects twice as far away. With ISO 25 film, the maximum shooting distance is only half that of the flash with ISO 100 film.

Flash photography If you are using a flashgun it is usually because there is not enough light to give you a shutter speed that will not result in camera shake. If the difference between the flash synchronization speed and the shutter speed the meter recommends for a given aperture in ambient light is more than two stops, you can effectively treat flash exposure calculation as if it were for exposure in a black room.

Below Fill-in flash permits dark subjects against a bright background (left) to receive enough exposure to render them more pleasing to the eye (right).

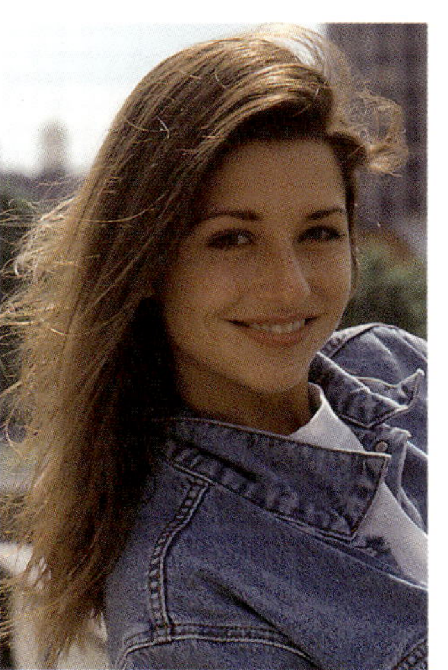

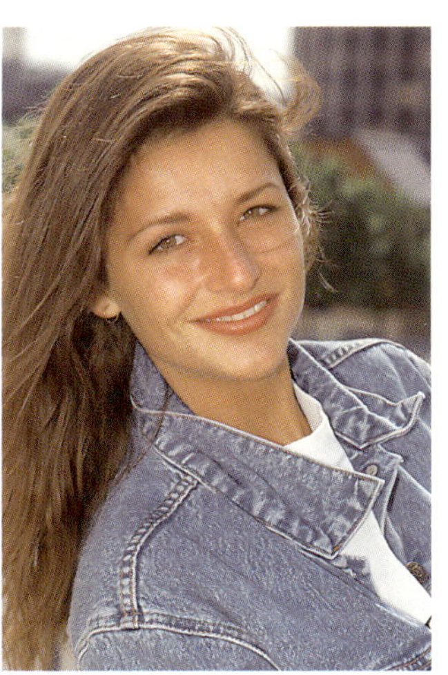

Fill-in flash If your meter recommends a useable shutter speed for a given aperture, it does not mean that flash is inappropriate. Where the light is coming from behind the subject, the exposure for the background might be correct, but the subject will be drastically underexposed. While it is possible to expose for the subject with careful metering, the result will be a washed-out background. The solution is to set a shutter speed and aperture combination that exposes the background correctly, and supplement the ambient light with a flash burst to 'fill in' the detail in the subject. The shutter speed selected should be the flash sync speed of the camera. It is unusual for absolutely no ambient light to fall on the subject, so give the subject less flash exposure than for a straight flash

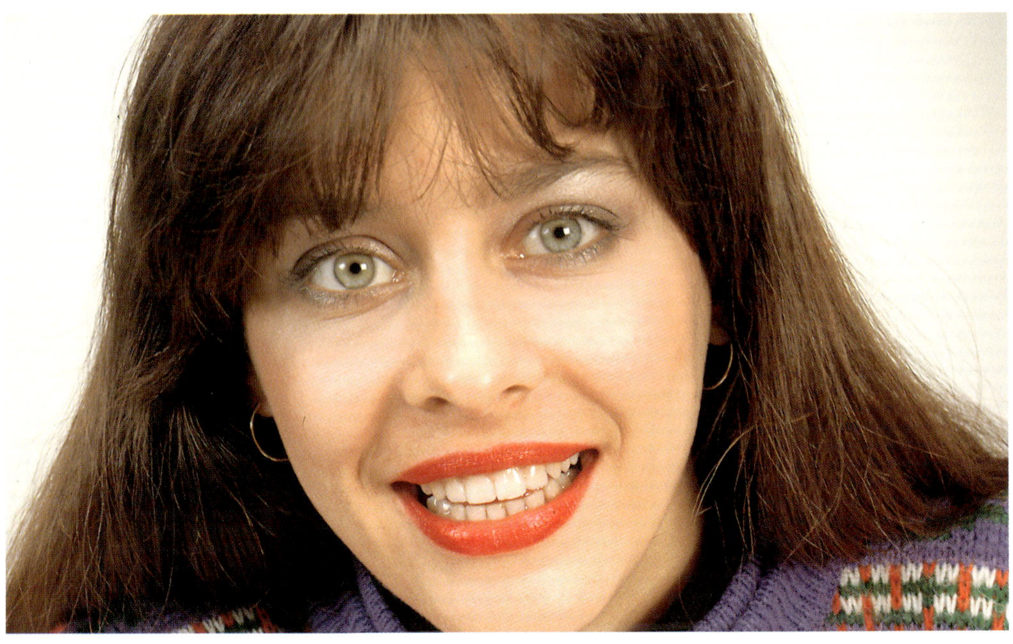

Above Using two flashes gives more even lighting to portraits – especially when diffused.
Below A useful second flash is a small gun with a slave unit; it allows cordless synchronization and thus more freedom of placement.

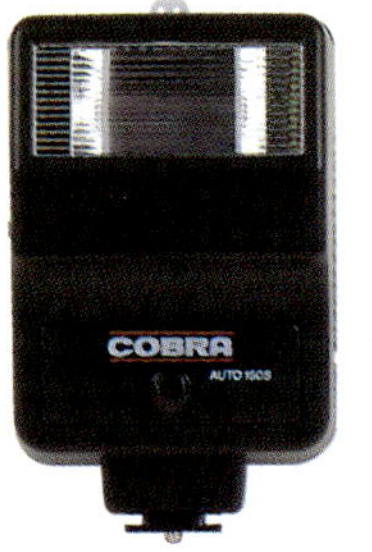

shot, by setting the film speed on the flashgun to one or two stops faster than the film being used.

Direct or bounce? The light from a flashgun is usually rather harsh, as are the shadows it generates; this will not retain detail in anything other than flat matt subjects. A solution is to use bounce flash, reflecting the light from the flash off another surface onto the subject. For portraits indoors, the most usual surface is a ceiling: point the head of the flashgun up so light bounces at the same angle from ceiling to flash as ceiling to subject.

The light from bounce flash is more diffuse than direct flash, but there are three drawbacks. Exposure must be calculated differently, as the subject/flash distance is increased and the reflecting surface will absorb one or two stops of light. Secondly, if the reflecting surface is not neutral in colour, the subject may be imbued with the tinge of that colour. Finally, light bounced off a ceiling may create shadows (albeit softer than direct flash), especially under eyebrows and nose.

One flash or two? To fill in shadows caused by bounce flash or for a slightly more creative lighting set-up, use a second, smaller, flashgun. Bear in mind how it will be triggered and how its additional light will affect the overall exposure. Triggering can be done either by an electrical pulse carried by a cable that plugs into the camera via a PC (power cord) socket or a special adaptor; or by a slave unit (built into a flashgun or in a separate unit) consisting of a light-sensitive cell that emits a triggering voltage to the second flashgun when it detects a flash burst.

Below More advanced guns can tilt and swivel, allowing you to obtain the quality and direction of light desired.

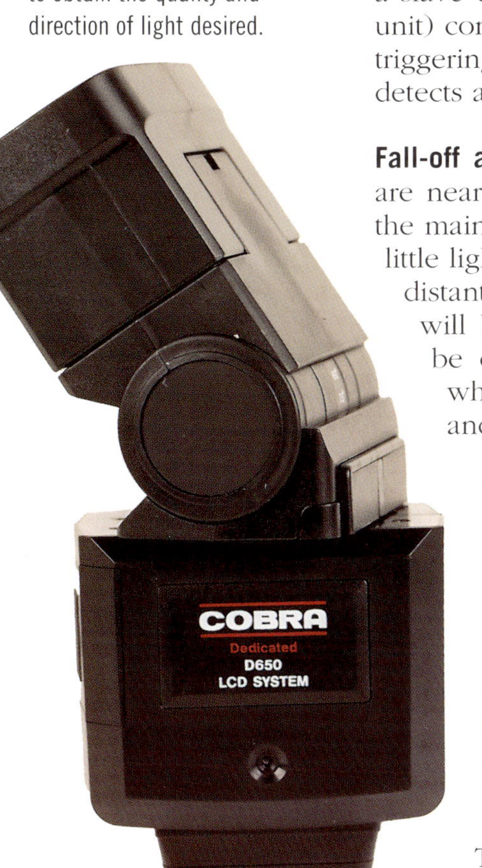

Fall-off and burn-out Where objects in the frame are nearer to or further away from the flash than the main subject, they will reflect too much or too little light back to the film. Where subjects are too distant and the flash light has 'fallen off', they will be underexposed. Subjects too close will be overexposed and bleach out to a bright white. Slide film is especially prone to fall-off and burn-out.

Redeye This is caused by the flash head and lens axis being close together, with the result that the subject's pupils appear bright red. There are three ways around this. You can take the flash away from the axis of the lens either by bouncing it off a ceiling or wall or by using a PC cord to remove it from the camera altogether; increase the ambient illumination; and try to reduce the diameter of the subject's pupils by firing a number of pre-flashes. The closer you are to a subject, the less likely it is that redeye will occur, as the angle between the flash and lens increases.

Steadying the Camera

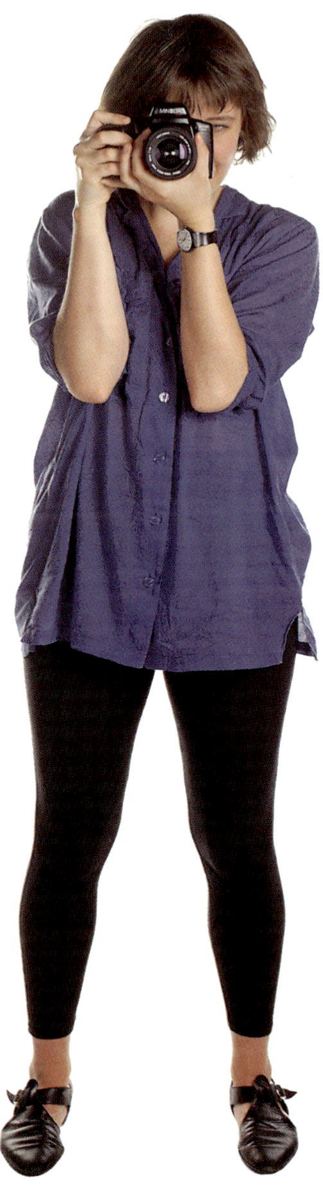

The human body is moving all the time, although we do not usually notice the minor everyday shakings and tremblings. Besides breathing, we shiver to keep warm, when scared or when over-stimulated by substances such as nicotine, tea and coffee. These body tremors are so small that it is only when we scrutinize slightly blurred photos just back from the lab that we have real (and unwanted) evidence on film, to prove we moved the camera during the exposure. This common picture fault is known as camera shake.

However, image blur is not always synonymous with camera shake. Subject movement during an exposure (especially when combined with poor focusing) looks very similar. Look through a magnifying glass at the subject and then at the background: if the immediate background is sharp, the causes are subject movement and a degree of poor focusing. Selecting a faster shutter speed or gentle panning in the same direction as your subject will help.

Brace yourself In terms of both finance and convenience, nothing can beat the fabulous human tripod! Elbows tucked into the body, hand cupped under the lens, legs straight, weight evenly distributed, and feet hip distance apart: breathe out gently (or hold your breath) before releasing the shutter.

To see how long you can hold the camera steady before encountering camera shake, attach a sheet of newspaper to a well-lit wall (perhaps beside a window, to control the amount of available light with the curtains). Using a 50mm standard lens on the camera and a slow film (so graininess will not interfere with the sharpness of your results), focus on the letters and change the shutter speed setting in one stop increments. Start making your handheld exposures at fast speeds (say 1/125sec), then with the curtains closed move on to the slower ones (such as 1/2sec and 1sec). Keep a written note of the film frame numbers and corresponding shutter speed

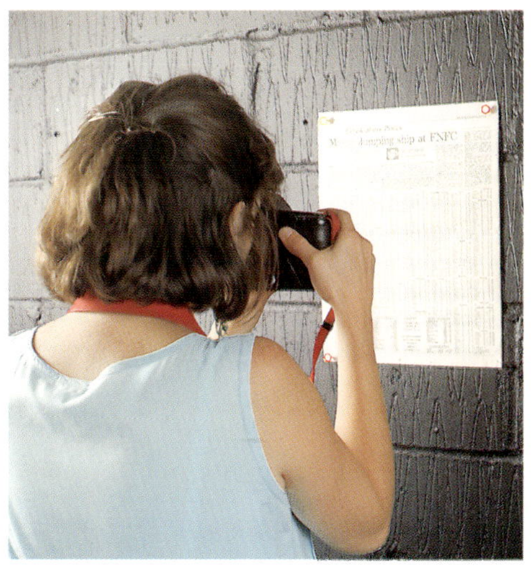

Above Use a sheet of newspaper to test how slow a speed you can use before encountering camera shake.

Diagnosing camera shake Using a magnifying glass, look for the following symptoms on your slides and negatives.

- Image completely blurred with nothing acceptably sharp in frame. The degree of blur illustrates how serious the camera shake problem is. (Do not be confused by the excessive graininess associated with fast films.)
- Unidirectional or rotational blurring. This occurs at the split second the shutter release button is depressed. Because the shutter release is located on one side of the camera body when you press it down this causes a slight and momentary loss of camera balance.
- Double images occur during long exposures. Check the number of outlines around small picture details such as eyebrows or specks from a bonfire.

Tripods By far the safest way to ensure a steady result is to avoid touching the camera altogether. Secure the camera to a tripod, then use a cable release, remote control or self-timer to release the shutter.

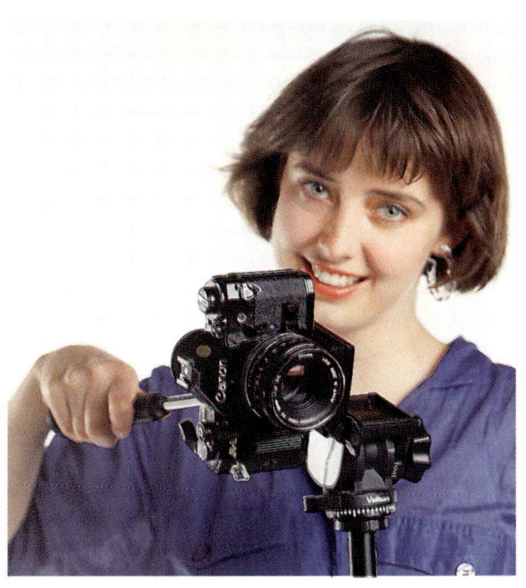

Below Tripod-mounting your camera ensures a steady result.

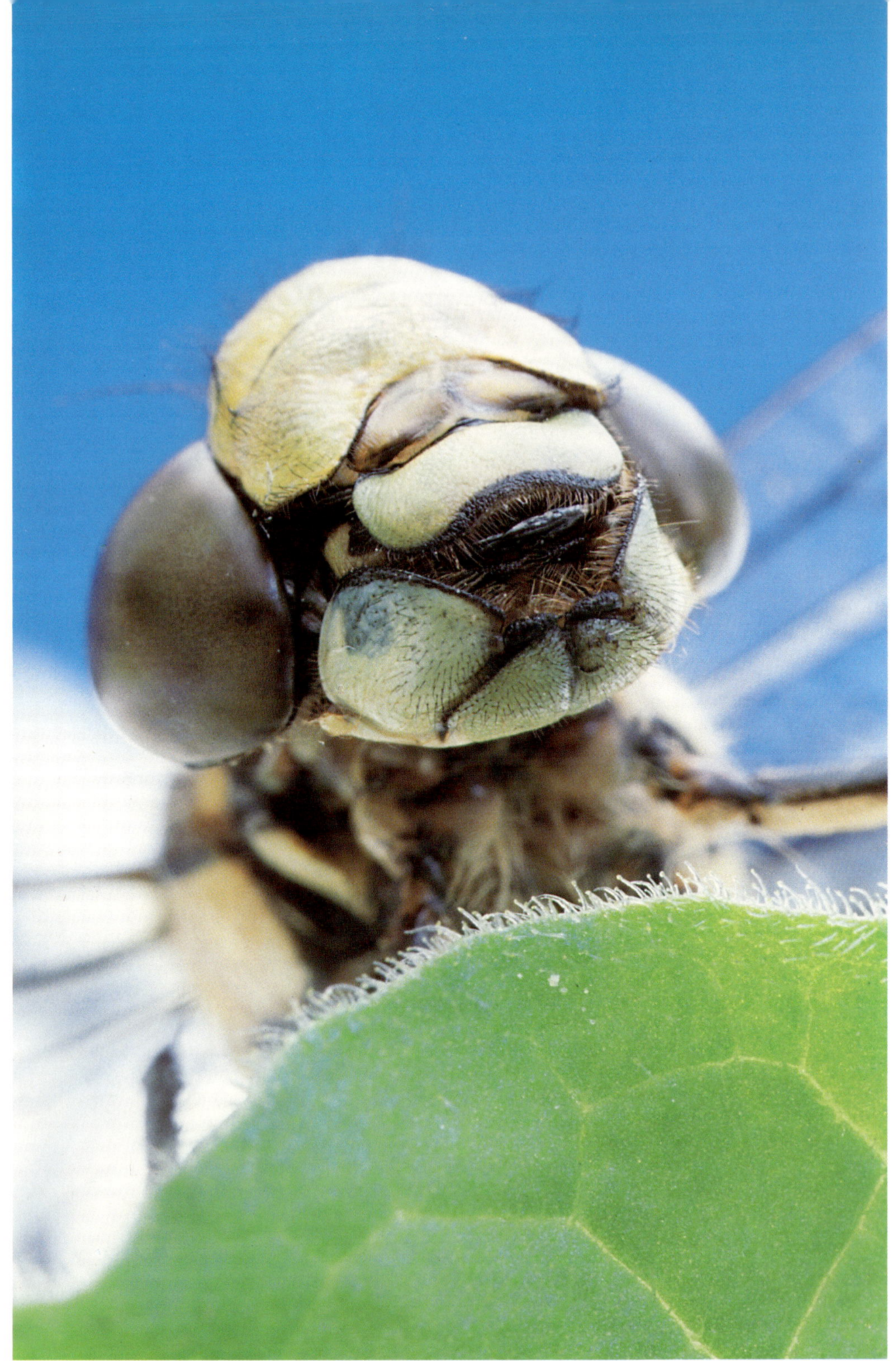

Steadying the Camera

Left Macro lenses have minimal depth of field, so accurate focusing can become a nightmare! Using a tripod leaves your hands free for focusing, allowing you to use slower shutter speeds – hence smaller aperture settings – for increased depth of field. This hoverfly was shot using a tripod and flash at f/16 on Kodachrome 64, with a 100mm macro lens.

Below Catching mist at dawn requires a slow shutter speed and a tripod, especially with a 75–300mm lens on the camera.

All photographic pursuits are made easier by improving camera steadiness because shutter speed restrictions are removed. Tripods give greater freedom in a number of ways, enabling you to use smaller aperture settings (thereby gaining increased depth of field), and slower films for finer-grain images, even on dull days. They allow you to focus more accurately when using a macro lens, as depth of field is minimal; to support telephoto lenses for longer periods, and thus isolate the action at sports events where access is restricted; and to make time exposures at night, blurring traffic and other movement with the shutter speed dial on 'B'. Using a tripod also gives you time to consider the image more carefully before you release the shutter, with the viewfinder becoming a more fixed reference point. Larger format cameras, usually studio-bound, become less unwieldy and easier to use with a tripod.

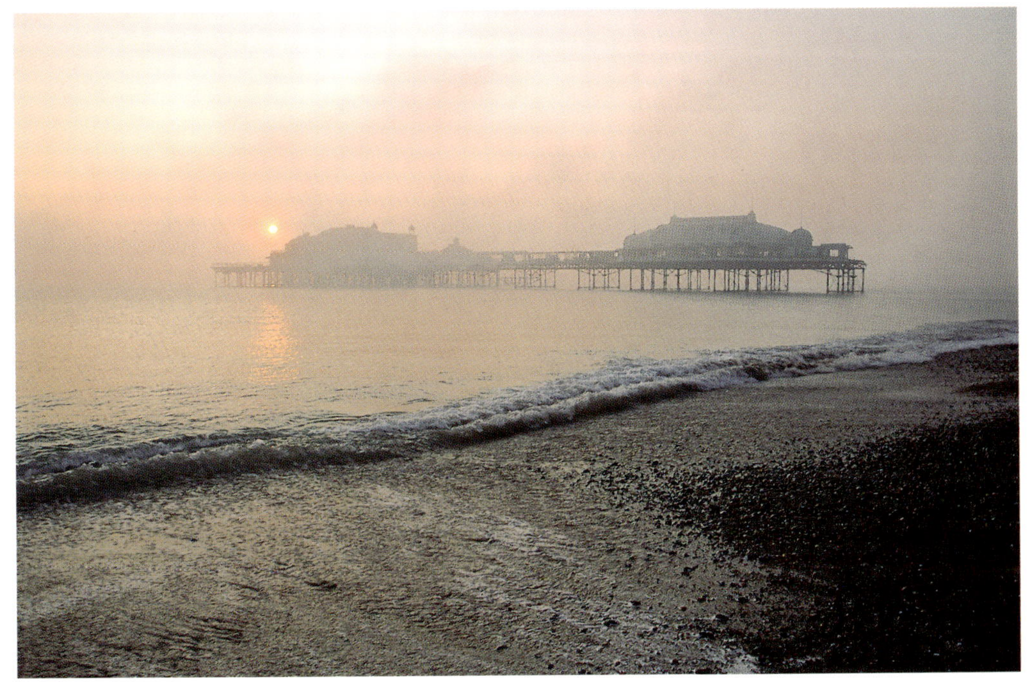

Composition

Once you have mastered the sciences of exposure and focusing, and understand the effects you can achieve with different focal length lenses, shooting distances, films and accessories, there is only one decision left to make – what goes in the viewfinder? There is no one correct way to photograph a scene, or photography would be very dull. Choosing how to interpret a scene – how to interplay all the elements – is a very personal decision.

The term 'composition' can be summed up by four questions you should ask yourself:

- What is the main subject?
- Where should I shoot from?
- Where should I place the subjects (by altering the angle of the camera)?
- How big should the main subject be in relation to the background?

Facing page Shooting from the bottom of a tall building with a wideangle lens exaggerates the perspective.
Below The same subject can be made to look different by getting closer and changing the angle of shooting.

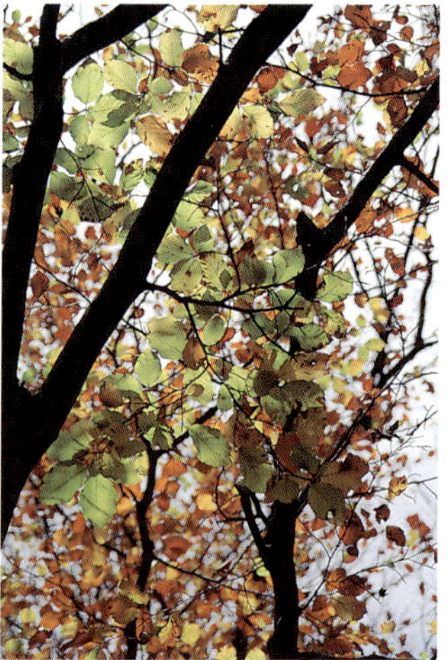

The answers to some of these questions will be determined by the physical factors at the scene, and some by the limitations of your equipment. However, there are also a range of compositional guidelines that can help you frame an attractive image.

Format One of the first and most basic things you need to decide on is whether you want a horizontal or a vertical image.

These are respectively known as landscape and portrait formats, as most pictures shot of a single

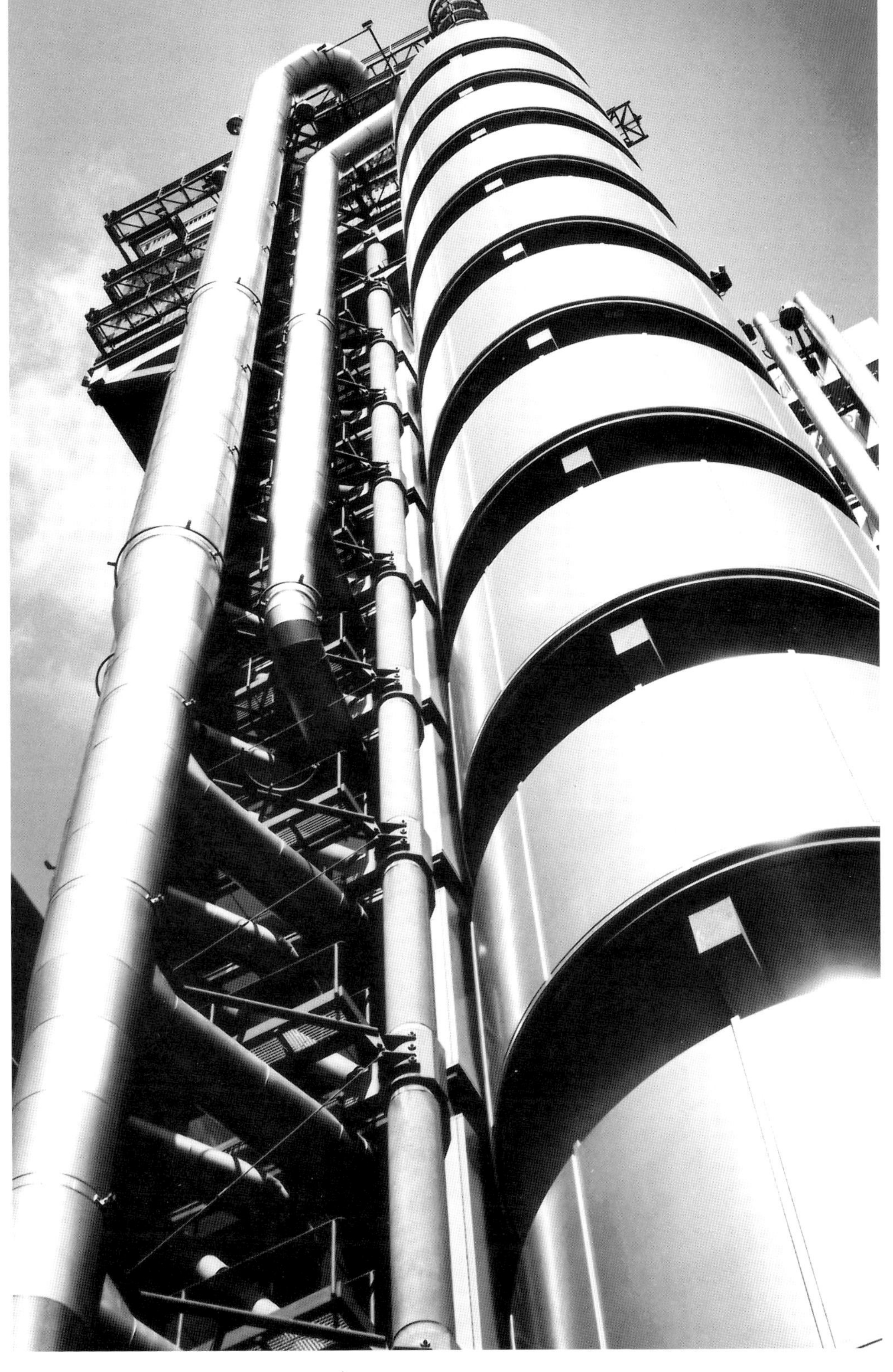

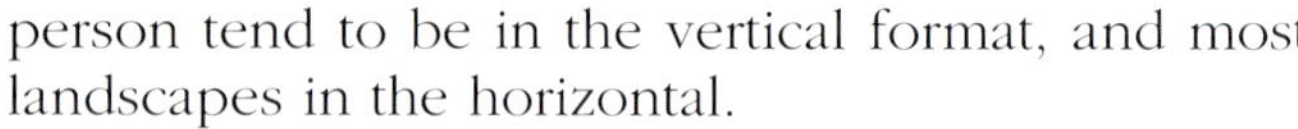

person tend to be in the vertical format, and most landscapes in the horizontal.

As with all 'rules', though, there are times when this does not hold true. Try shifting from horizontal to vertical framing when looking at a shot to see which works best; the change can be surprisingly dramatic.

Shooting position Using your feet changes how a scene looks. Although the brain recognizes a constantly changing scene as you move, a photograph freezes the balance of foreground and background. By moving around you can alter the balance until you get an appealing composition.

Below Positioning a subject at the point of intersection of thirds can make an attractive composition. The subject below has a diagonal leading from bottom left to top right, making it especially effective.

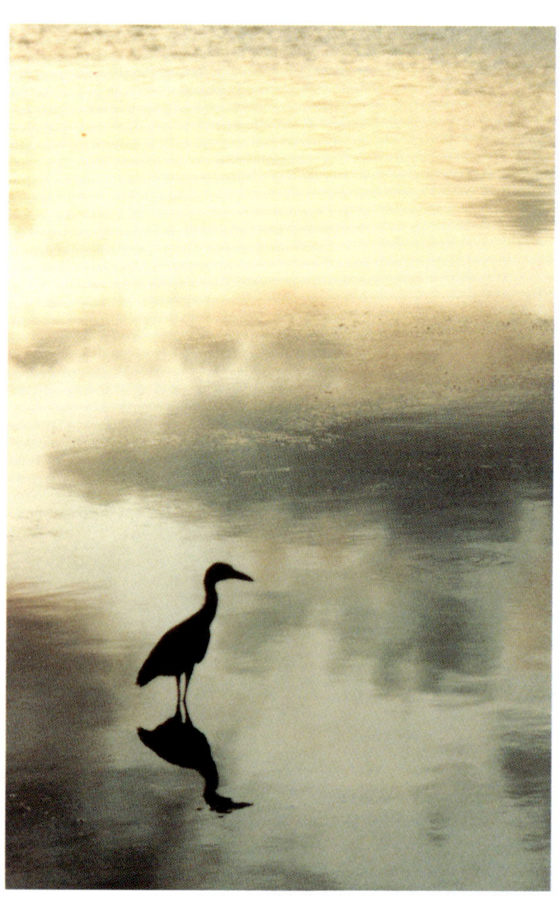

Rule of thirds Your subject does not need to be at the dead centre of your picture, but it should not be placed randomly: the 'rule of thirds' is a compositional aid to help you judge the most pleasing or dramatic position for the subject and the overall aesthetic effect of your photograph.

Plainly stated, the rule says that on an imaginary grid of nine equal-sized rectangles laid over a picture, any element of the picture that appears at any of the corners of the central rectangle will have maximum compositional impact. Use this to compose a powerful shot.

Horizons Until you start looking hard at scenes and considering them through the viewfinder of a camera, you tend to take it for granted that the horizon runs across the middle of a scene.

Changing the balance of sky to ground can radically affect the look of a scene. Almost filling the frame with the sky gives the impression of wide open plains. But if you leave only a thin strip of sky at the top of a scene you will just crowd the view.

Horizons need not always be straight, nor is the natural horizon of a shot always the junction of sky and land. Where there is a large expanse of water that reflects the scene beyond it, the natural horizon of the shot is the junction of the water and land, or the water and sky. This horizon can also be moved up or down for artistic effect.

Shots with an undulating horizon can have much more impact than flat scenes, especially if a strong subject breaks the join.

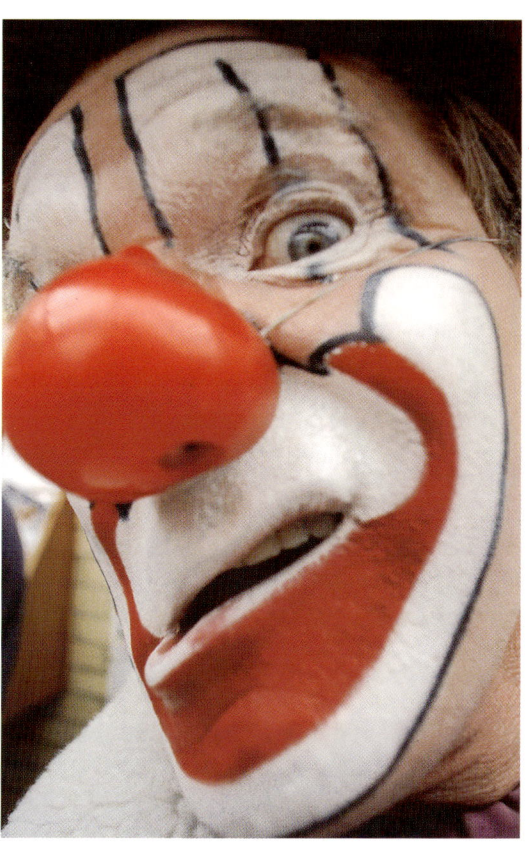

Leading lines Lines that lead the viewer's eye into or across the picture are very useful compositional tools. Normally these take the form of converging lines which can be physical – like the edge markings of a road – or implied – like shadows.

Be different Often the most impressive shots are those that do not immediately spring to mind as obvious subjects. There is nothing wrong with picturing a scene that instinctively calls out for a photograph, but there may be other shots that could be taken other than by approaching from in front and shooting parallel to the ground. Moving in closer than expected often has an interesting effect.

Above This closely cropped portrait shows how composing tightly about a powerful or dramatic face increases the impact of the shot.

Next page A restful, harmonious composition that makes excellent use of converging diagonal lines.

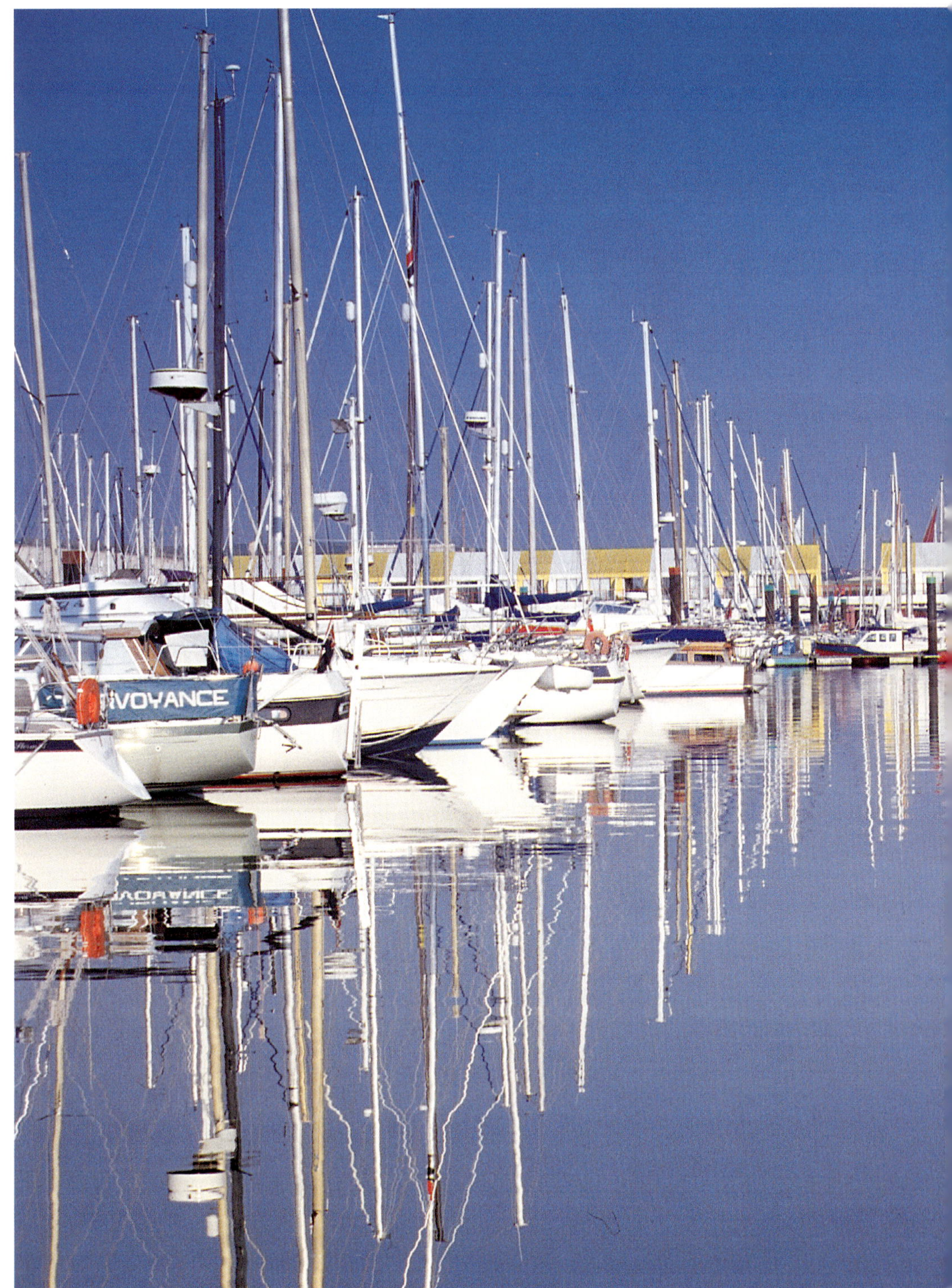
VOYANCE

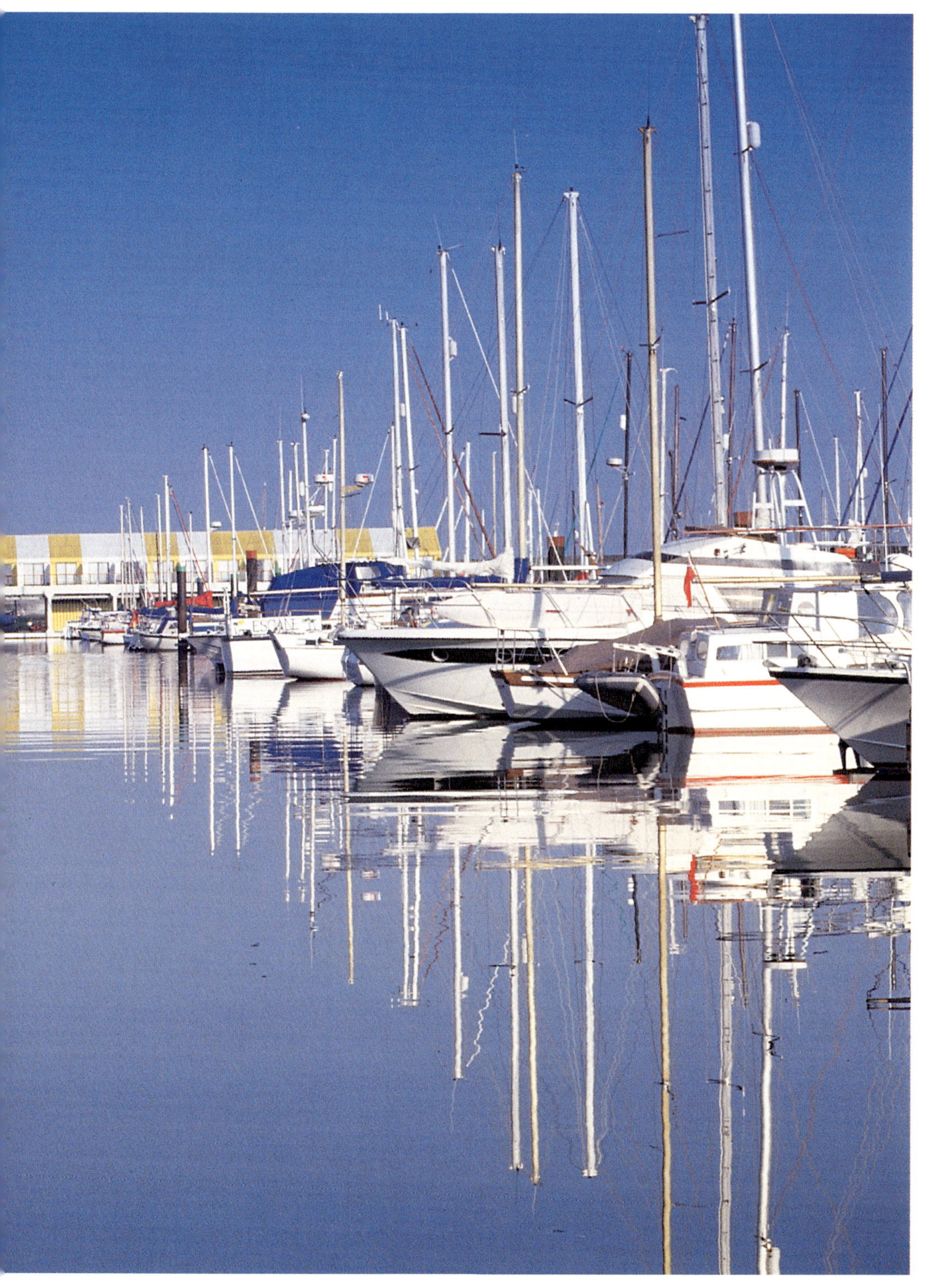

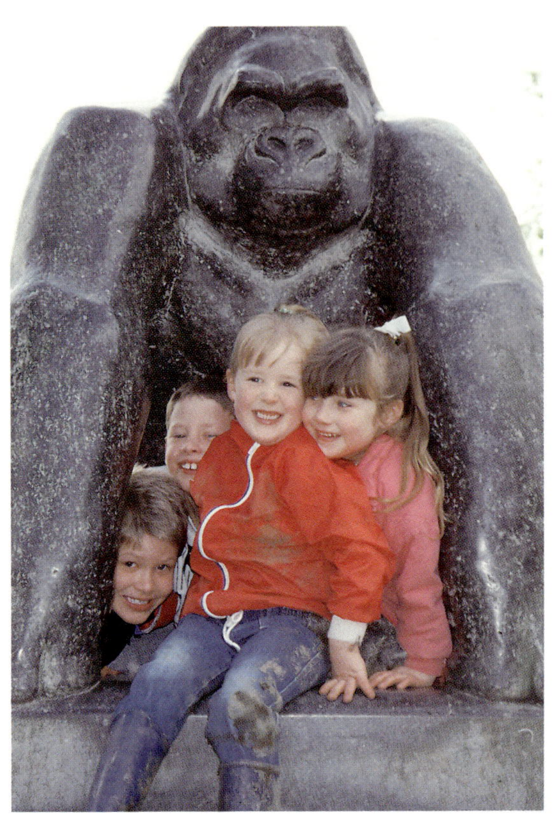

Above Including a subject of known size on a monumental subject allows the viewer to judge just how large it is.
Facing page Deliberately getting the perspective of a scene wrong can often make for a powerful composition.

Keep it simple The compositional guidelines given here should give you a few ideas on how to approach a subject, but you cannot apply all these ideas to one scene. In some circumstances, the best rule is to keep it simple. If there are too many points of interest in a picture, it is very difficult for the viewer to take in. Generally, the more crowded a picture is, the less interesting it becomes.

To get your compositional spurs, try concentrating on getting just one point of interest, and maximizing impact. Note that maximizing a subject's impact does not always mean making it big.

Framing If your subject has a particularly strong shape, filling the frame with the subject – either by using a longer focal length lens or by getting closer to it – will emphasize that shape and make for a stronger picture.

Picture scale Very often the key to a strong composition is a relatively plain picture whose generally smooth look is broken by a small point of interest. With landscapes or monument shots, enhance the impact of the shot by making an object of known size the point of interest, to give a sense of scale.

Colour One method of increasing the impact of a picture is by making part of the scene stand out from the background. Apart from selective focusing, using a narrow depth of field, the main way

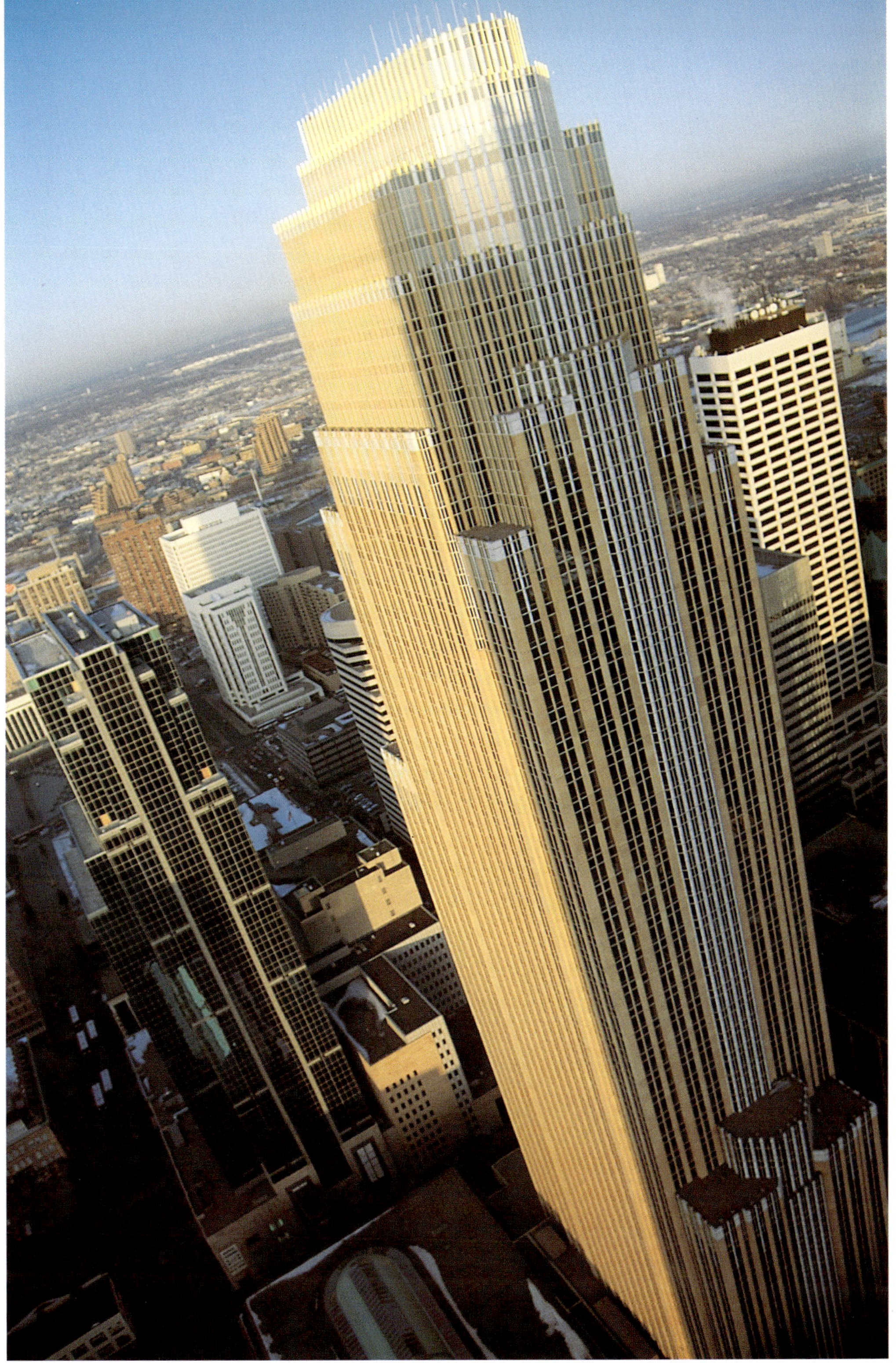

of achieving this is to have a subject whose colour or tone is radically different from the background. This colour separation is further enhanced by which colours you use. Reds and yellows will seem to come out of the picture, while blues, browns and greens tend to recede into it. Placing a red subject against a blue background will make the subject jump out of the shot.

Number of subjects Depending on what type of subjects you are shooting, you can emphasize one in particular or give them all equal importance. By arranging the subjects in recognizable shapes, you will cause the viewer's eye to travel from one to another in a simple, seamless way. For example, placing a trio of subjects in a straight line will have less impact than placing them in a triangle. Putting the point of the triangle at the top of the picture reinforces the brain's idea of convergent lines disappearing to a point at infinity. Place the point of the triangle at the base of the picture, and the scene will take on an unstable look which can disturb the eye but make for an interesting shot.

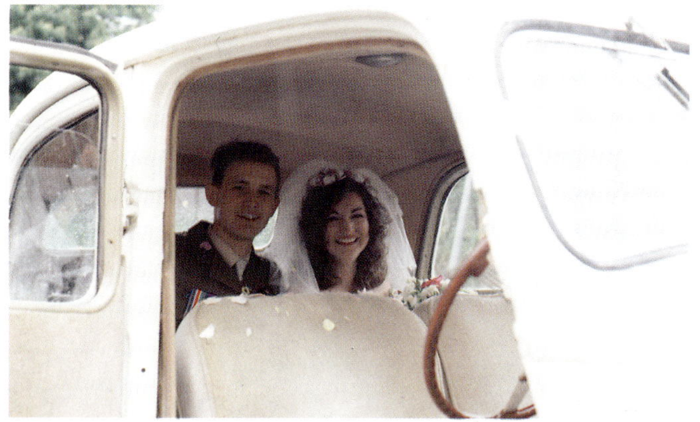

Left Using a frame that complements the subject helps to put a picture in context.

Natural frames When looking through the view-finder to frame a subject, you may spot an existing part of the scene that will frame it for you. This could be the arch of a bridge, or a silhouetted piece of architecture framing a tower in full sunlight, or the branches of an overhanging tree. Natural frames can give an impression of depth to a scene, as well as pleasingly setting off the subject.

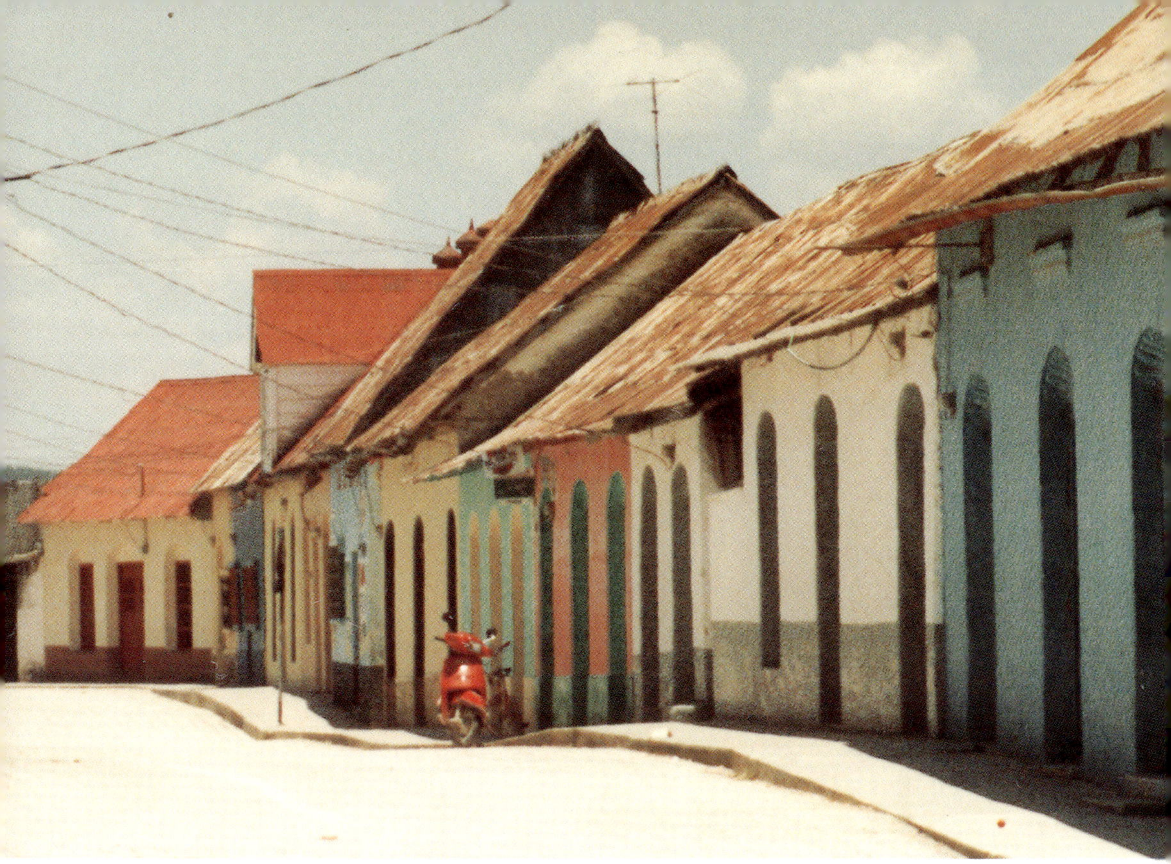

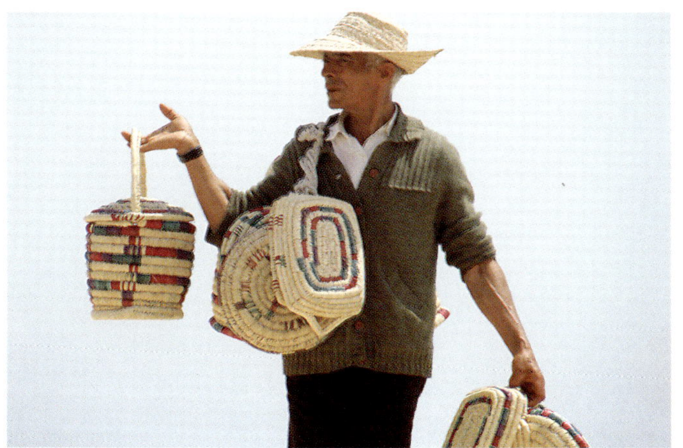

Above Triangular compositions can lead the eye in and out of a picture, in this case from the pavement through to the last house, then along the roof to the top right of the image.
Left The bags at the end of this vendor's arms form two points of a triangle, with his head at the apex.

Portraits

The word 'portrait' may generate images of old masters' oils hanging on a gallery wall, but in photography it amounts to no more than deliberately taking a picture of someone.

So what are the ground rules for portraiture? The secret of a successful portrait lies in having a clear idea of what you want to do. The control you assume over the selection, position, number, treatment and lighting of your subject(s) will largely determine the style and quality of the shot you take.

Facing page The essence of candid photography is catching a fleeting expression on film, as with this youngster caught in mid-sulk.

Below How not to make friends with your sitter. Lit from below with undiffused flash and shot from very close with an ultra-wideangle lens.

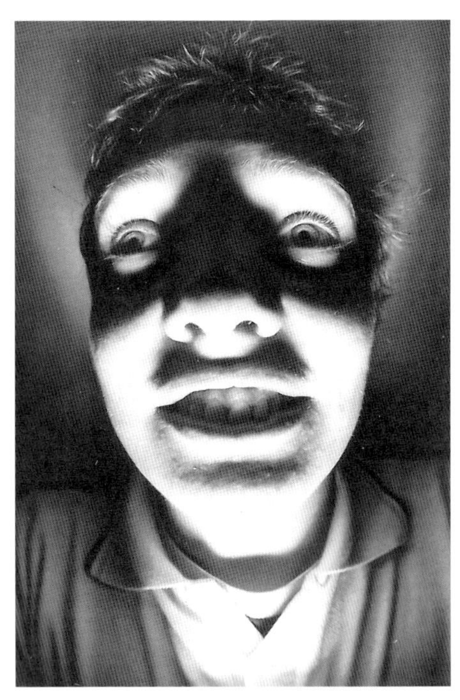

Who is it for? There is a big difference between taking a picture for someone else than for your own pleasure. If the picture is for the sitter, you probably need to make them look good – or at least as good as they think they look. Few people think they resemble their pictures. Most of us have a self-image based on a laterally reversed, life-sized image, viewed from about a foot away – that is, a mirror's reflection. The truth is, sitters will look the way you want them to look.

Good candids The ideal example of this is candid photography. Dictionary definitions of candid are 'completely sincere' or 'severely critical'. In photography, this means either picturing people in an everyday activity or while they are making fools of themselves.

Generally a good candid shot occurs in two ways. You can grab a moment in time on film before your prey has a chance to react, or you can anaesthetize

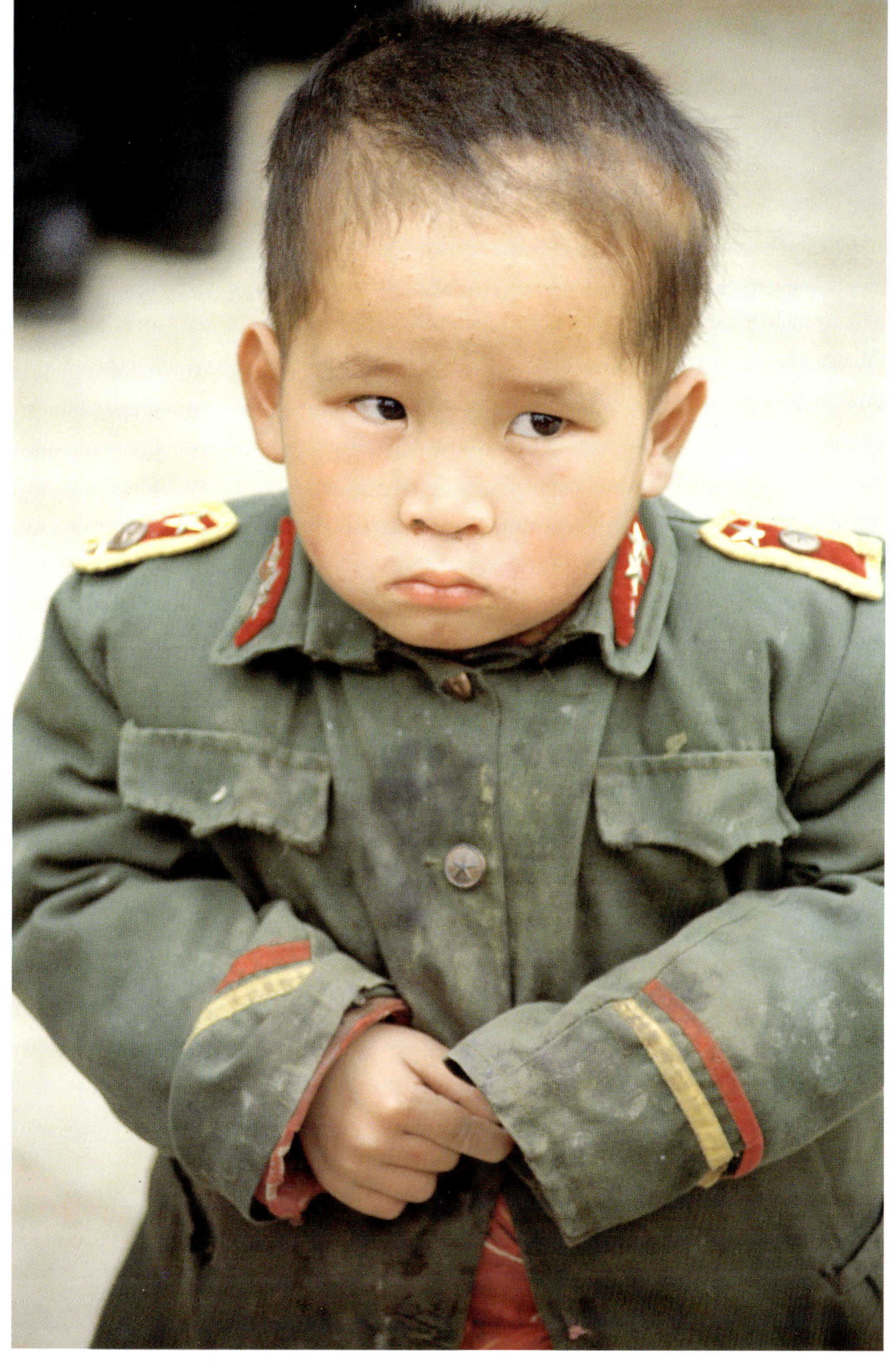

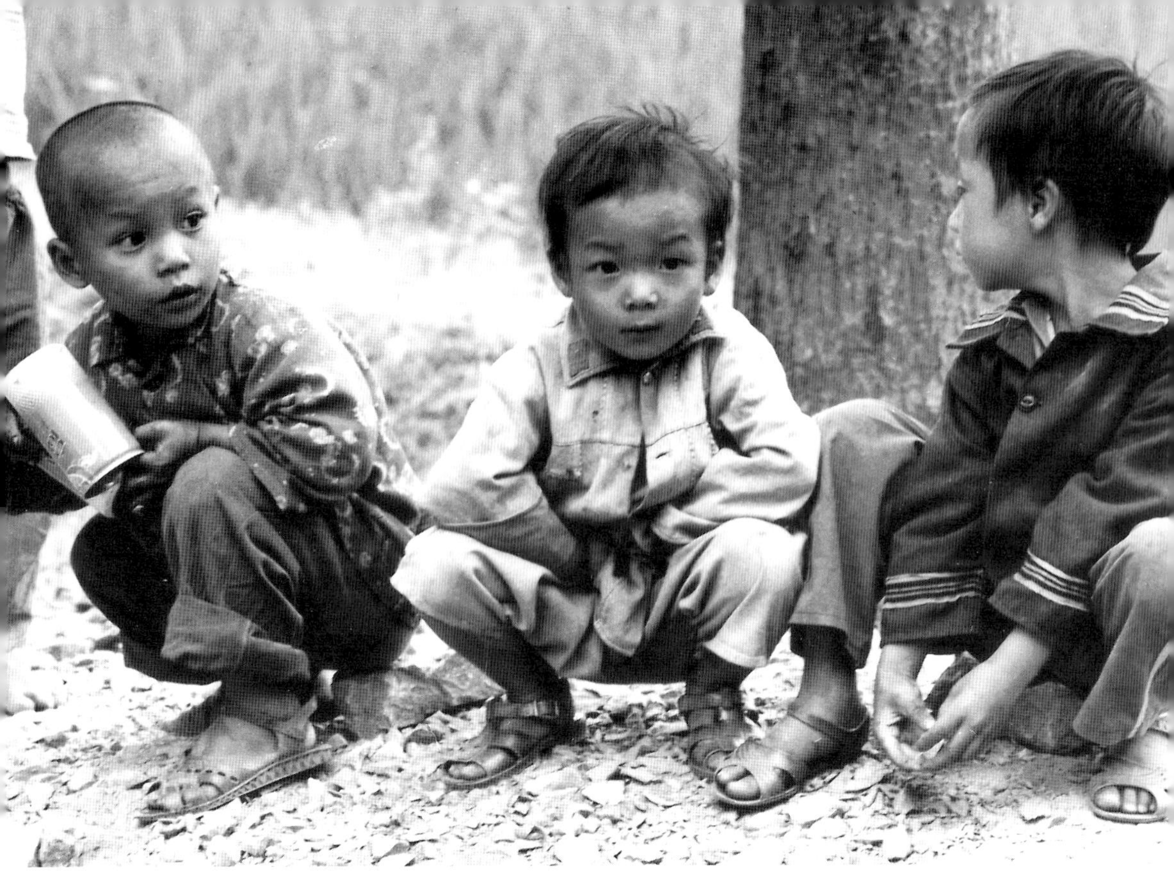

Above Hang around with a camera for a while, and children will forget you are there.
Below Close cropping can produce a very effective and often unusual portrait.

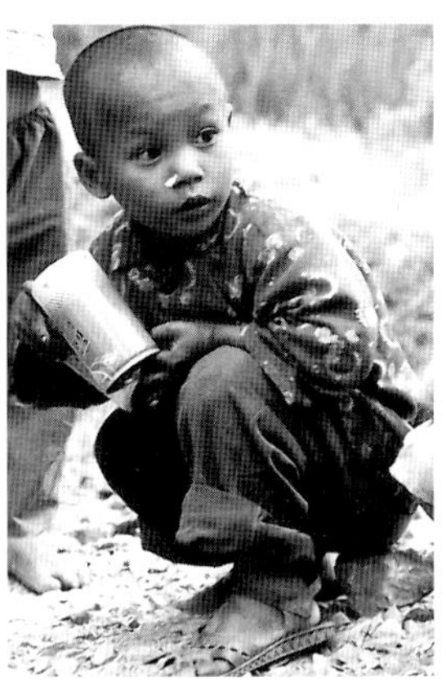

the subject to the danger of a camera in their presence by toting it around until they lose their self-consciousness. Children love to play to the camera but they have a low boredom threshold and will soon forget you are there.

Key questions If someone knows you are going to take their picture, you must seize control. Once you are spotted it is pointless saying, 'Imagine I'm not here'. But with this inevitable element of formality there comes the problem of how you want the picture to be taken. The key questions you should ask yourself before taking a portrait are:

- Should I shoot in the horizontal or vertical format? The answer depends on the subject's pose.
- How big in the viewfinder do I want the subject, and how much of the body do I want to include in the frame?
- How far away do I need to be and which lens do I need to use to achieve this?

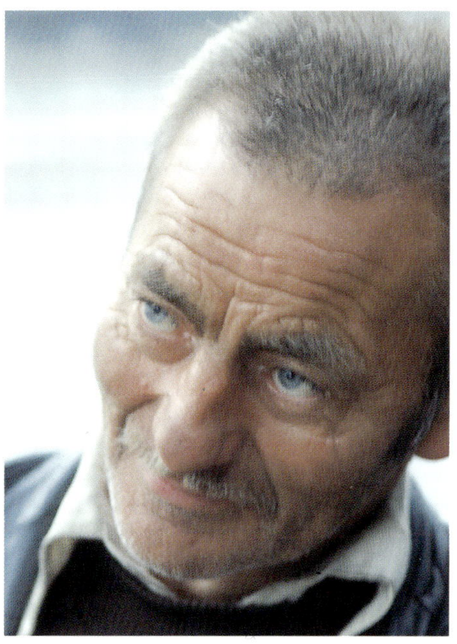

Above When the subject looks away from the camera, the effect can often be as powerful as a direct gaze.

- What kind of background should I use, how much should of it be included in the frame and how sharp should it be? This last factor will often depend on the lens in use and the shooting distance. Unless the background is relevant to the portrait, get rid of it by using a wide aperture. This also allows a faster shutter speed to be used, reducing the possibility of camera shake.
- Where should I focus? Almost without exception the answer is ... on your subject's eyes. If your subject has a prominent nose and you focus on it while leaving the rest of the face out of focus, you will not be very popular!
- Where should the subject be looking? This depends on the sitter, but wherever you ask your subject to look, get them to glance that way at the last moment, otherwise they will end up looking like a rabbit frozen by the glare of headlights.

If you are asking someone to look directly into the lens, experiment with the position of their head. Should they be looking down their nose, under their eyebrows, from one side or square on to the camera?

- From what height should I shoot? This is a question few people ask, but it is a very important one. Shoot from below if you want to give an impression of strength and power, from above for a feeling of vulnerability about the picture, or straight ahead for a 'normal' view. For child photography, getting down to hip height could well constitute 'normal' height for them. Changing the vertical position of the camera should also allow you to prevent the subject's head from being bisected by the top of a hedge or a horizon.
- What expression do I want the sitter to wear? As with eye contact, getting the expression to

appear a fraction of a second before the shot should ensure spontaneity. Many studio photographers guarantee a relaxed result by making their models pull funny faces before asking them to adopt the one wanted for the picture.

- It is important that you keep a dialogue going with your subject. Simply barking out orders is unlikely to result in anything but stilted and hackneyed photographs.

Handling groups Directing a single sitter is not too tricky, but the more people you want to photographs, the less likely it is that all of them will be following your instructions – at least not at the same time.

Preparation is once again most important. The cardinal sin of group portrait photography is to arrange the group to your satisfaction and then start choosing your lens, testing for exposure and deciding on film. Get all this sorted out before calling the group to order. Tripod-mounting the camera and using a longish cable release to trigger it will let you shoot at any moment, whether you are looking through the viewfinder or not.

Below Good use of foreground lets the viewer see what is holding the child's interest.

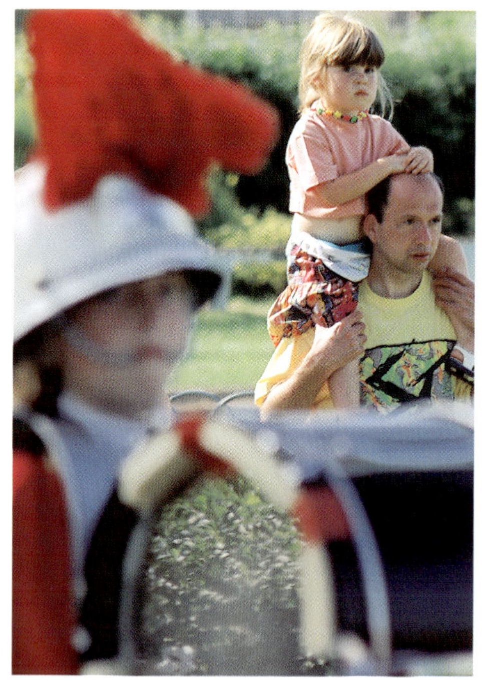

Ask your group to say a word like 'aspidistra' as you take the shot, or ask them all to count down aloud from five to one, and shoot when they get to three. Both these dodges guarantee audience participation from the group and hopefully they will show their teeth – not always easy – in a natural 'uncheesy' manner.

Arranging groups is not always easy in compositional terms. Try a couple of variations of each shot to get the best result. For example if there are, say, ten people of vastly different

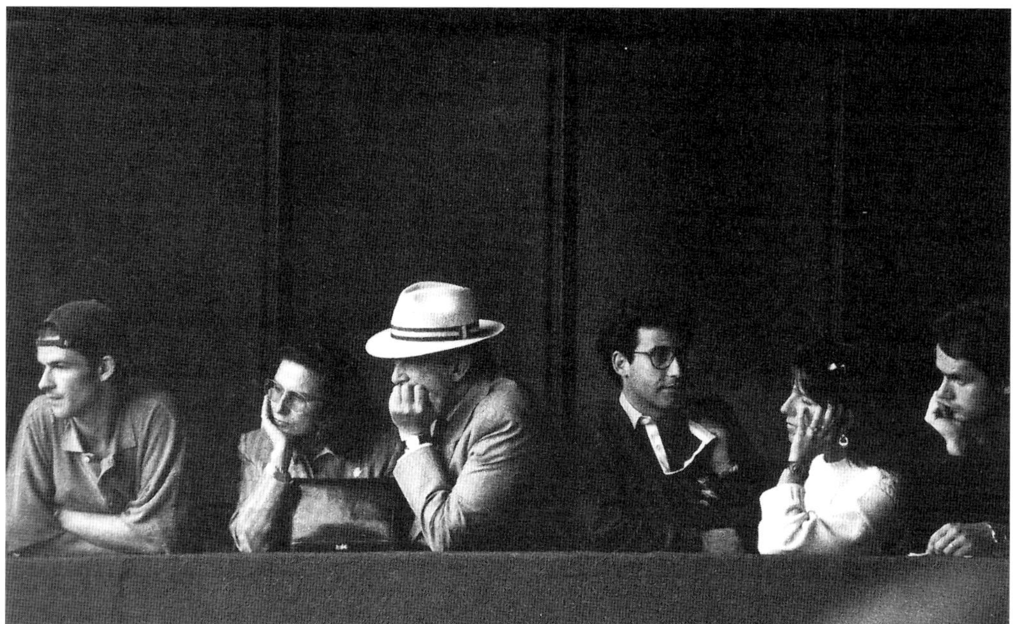

heights in the group, why not line them up in order of ascending height and shoot with a medium-wide focal length lens (35mm) from nearer those at the shorter end?

Above Subjects do not have to be looking in the same direction for a good candid image or informal portrait.

Choosing film Depending on the result you want, a prime consideration is your choice of film. Do you want to reproduce every pore in crisp detail? Do you want to enhance a diffused look with grainy film? What is the lighting set-up being used? Will you be shooting indoors or outdoors? Should you choose colour or mono film?

Mistakes to avoid There are 1001 mistakes you can make when shooting a portrait, but the main ones to avoid are:

- a subject's holding a pose for more than the minimum possible time.
- shooting only one picture. With almost all SLR cameras you do not see the moment of exposure

as the mirror flips up. During that instant anything may have happened. Most often it is the moment the sitter blinks.

- including a distracting background. Choosing too small an aperture will render the background sharp and draw attention away from the subject.
- Placing a subject too close to a background when using flash. This makes deeply distracting black shadows fall on the background.
- redeye. To get around it, use natural light where the situation allows, diffuse the flash or move the flash away from the camera (if possible).
- poor in-camera cropping. There is nothing wrong with filling the frame with the subject's head, but if you need to crop vertically to fill the frame, crop from the top down – otherwise your subject ends up with a disproportionately large forehead and no chin.
- backlighting. Unless you want a silhouette, do not shoot against bright light without putting some light onto the subject, or using fill-in flash.

Using perspective Shooting distance can radically alter the relative size of facial and body features. Shooting from a long distance (with a telephoto lens) can deemphasize certain facial features to create a more pleasant look for angular faces. On the other hand, even someone with drop-dead good looks can be made to look like a camel if you get close enough with an ultra-wideangle lens.

A mild telephoto lens (about 100mm focal length) allowing head and shoulder shots at about three metres is generally

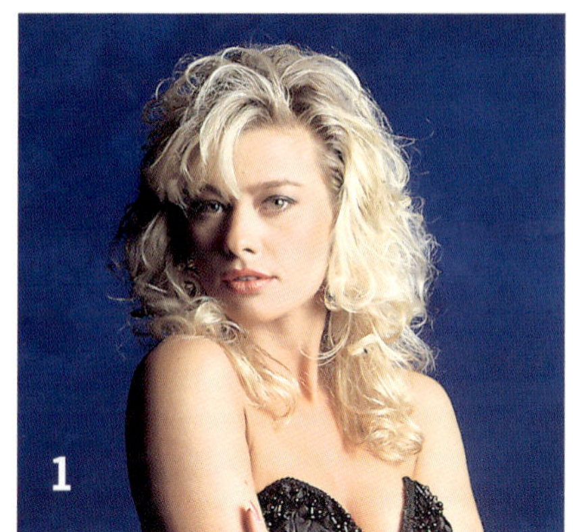
1

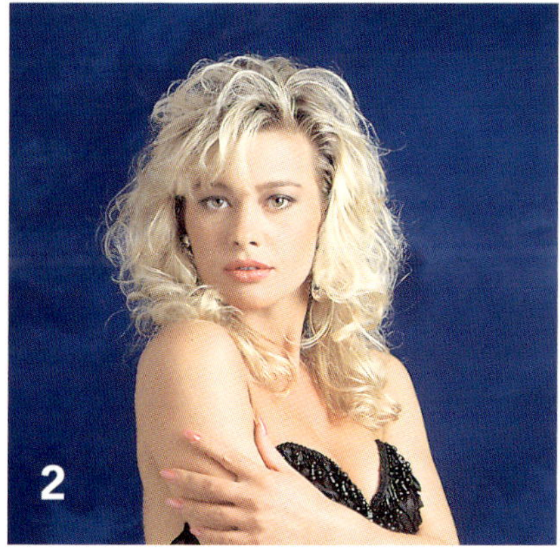
2

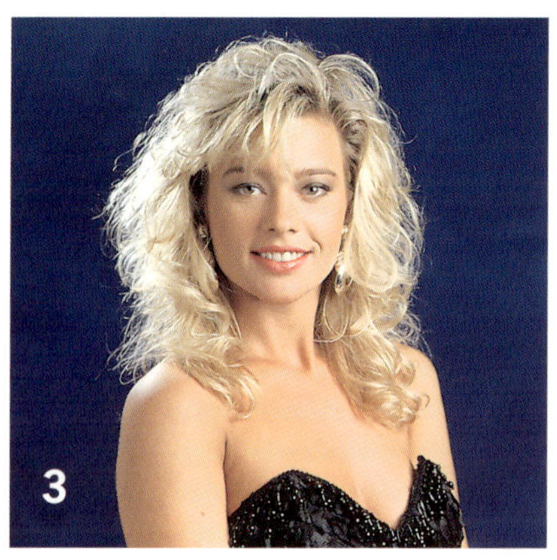
3

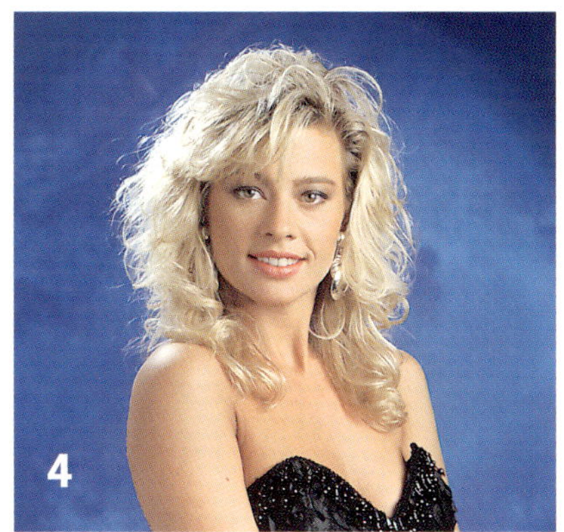

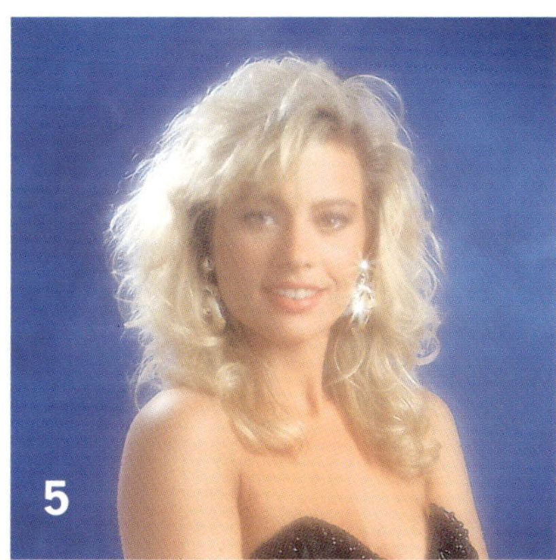

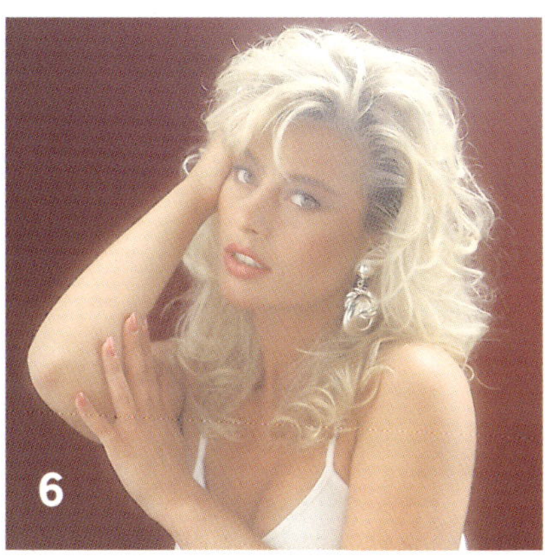

considered best to balance complimentary perspective with ease of shooting.

Studio shooting To get absolute control of portraiture, you cannot beat the studio. Light is controllable and does not change from second to second, so you do not have to change the exposure unless you want to. This frees you to concentrate on directing the sitter. You can also choose any background you wish to picture the sitter against. As lighting, and thus aperture, are completely under your control, these can be rendered sharp or defocused.

The number and position of lights, reflectors and filters you use can radically affect the shot, as the pictures on this page illlustrate.

1 A single flash high up to the right of the sitter leaves harsh shadows.
2 Adding a fill-in flash or a reflector to the lower left of the sitter gives a flatter, more complimen tary look.
3 Especially with blonde subjects, a light behind the sitter highlights the hair.
4 Another light played onto the background sepa rates the sitter from it and creates a less moody atmosphere.
5 Putting a standard starburst filter over the lens diffuses soft highlights and makes jewellery sparkle.
6 In this shot the only light was a bright softbox – a powerful diffused light – placed behind the subject. The camera was behind a huge piece of card covered in a crinkled sheet of gold-coloured foil and the lens hooded to prevent flare. The result is a soft, warm and very even light which highlights the hair effectively.

Landscapes

There is far more to taking a truly excellent landcape shot than merely recording your first impressions. Compared to portraits, landscapes are both easier and harder to shoot; and for the same reason.

With portraits, the main subject is mobile and near, so you can rearrange the elements in a scene either by moving the sitter or by moving the camera slightly. With landscape photography, the elements in a scene are a great deal less manoeuvrable, and generally a lot further away – so moving the camera does not allow you to make huge alterations to composition.

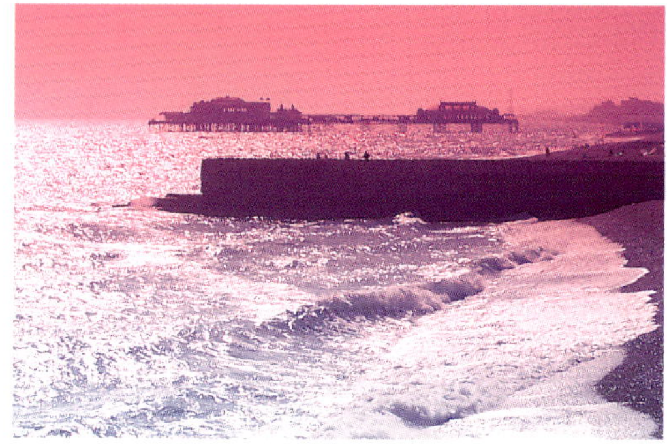

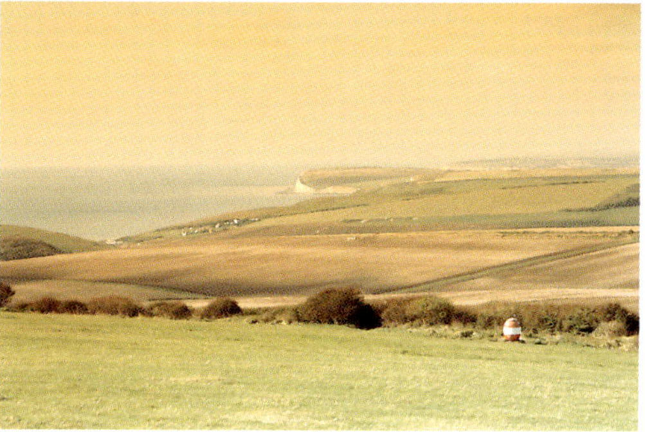

Filters Colours do not always occur naturally when you want them, and often a filter will pep up a good landscape shot into a really punchy one. Graduated filters are often the best choice as you will rarely want to alter the colour of both sky and foreground. Tobacco and pink graduates can create a sunset look, while a grey graduate lowers the contrast between a bright sky and less brightly illuminated foreground to coax maximum colour from both. Graduated blue filters enliven blue skies (although they can make clouds in the scene a little blue), as can polarizing filters, which reduce the amount of light coming from the sky, deepening its colour.

Above, top A graduated pink at the top and violet filter at the bottom create a serene atmosphere.

Above, bottom A graduated blue filter perks up the sky above this crop field to contrast against the golden glow.

How much sky? Possibly the most powerful way of affecting the mood of a photograph is by altering the balance of sky to land – that is, moving the horizon.

To convey a sense of wide open spaces, include more sky in a scene. Try flipping the camera through 90° into the vertical format, allowing you to place more sky in the frame. Vertically framed halfway horizons also look less static than horizontal 'landscape' format ones. In general, placing the horizon in the dead centre of a picture kills the mood. Often the only exception is when there is a flat expanse of water in the foreground which reflects the scene, creating a second, softer horizon and allowing you to place a horizon at each third of the scene. The main thing to ensure with horizons is that they are horizontal. It looks awful if a lake at the base of a range of hills is sloping from one side to the other.

Below 'Big' skies can imply a great sense of freedom when the weather is right.

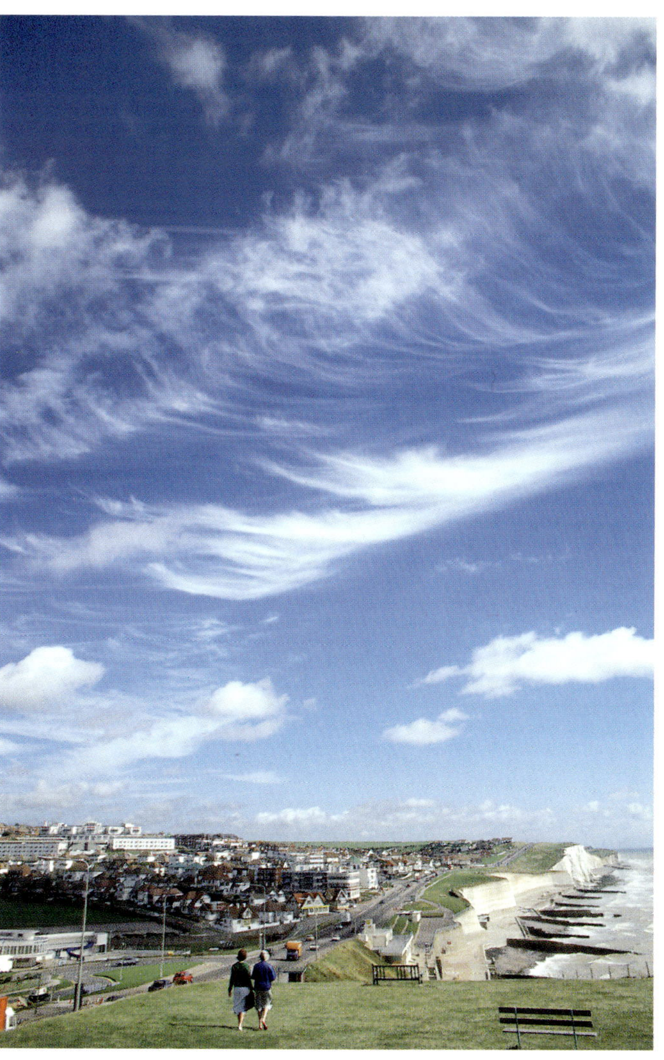

Harsh and soft Landscapes are radically affected by the quality and quantity of light. In strong lighting, shadows are deeper, contrast much higher and colours more saturated. But landscapes are not always best served by this kind of lighting. In particular, the overhead

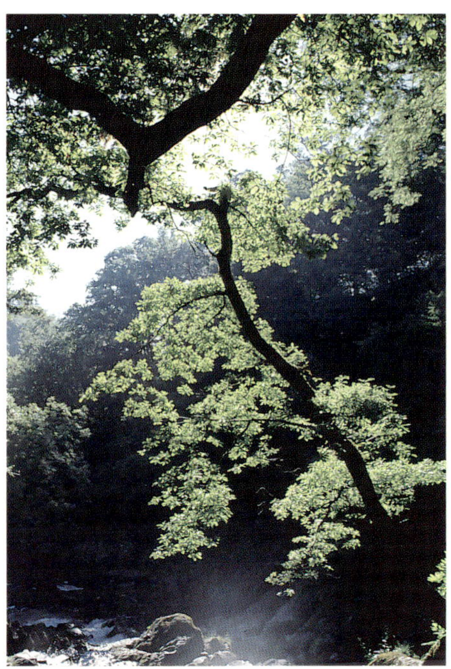

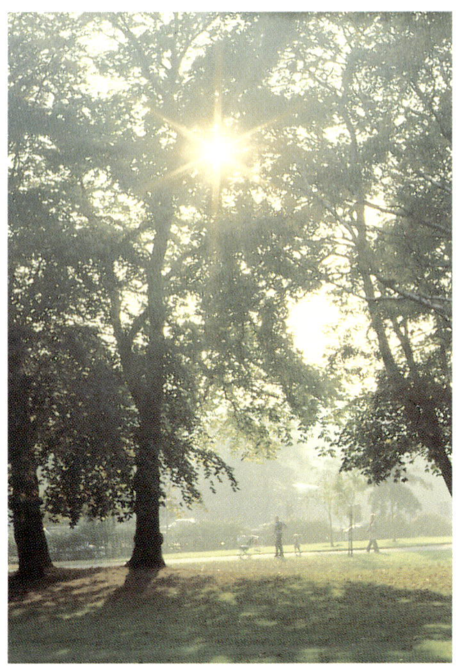

Above, left and right Times of day and times of year can markedly influence the qualities of the final shot, the strength of colours and the sharpness of subjects. Compare the crisp Spring light on the left with the Autumn diffusion.

Facing page Seascapes can follow a different set of rules from landscapes. In this calm Caribbean scene, reflection of a muted sky is what makes the picture.

light of the midday sun is too harsh, casting only very short shadows and leaving landscapes flat and featureless. It is often best to shoot with a slower shutter speed (stabilizing the camera on a tripod or wall) when there is less light around and it is heavily diffused: usually in the early morning or evening.

The sun The position of the sun in the sky alters the look of the scene. It is rarely a good idea to include the sun in the frame as the amount of light coming from it will cause the camera to underexpose the rest of the scene, while if you expose for the rest of the scene, you will be left with a white patch in the frame. The obvious exceptions to this rule are when the picture is taken as the sun is either rising or setting, or when it is partially obscured by an object in the frame, leaving shafts of sunlight filtering through.

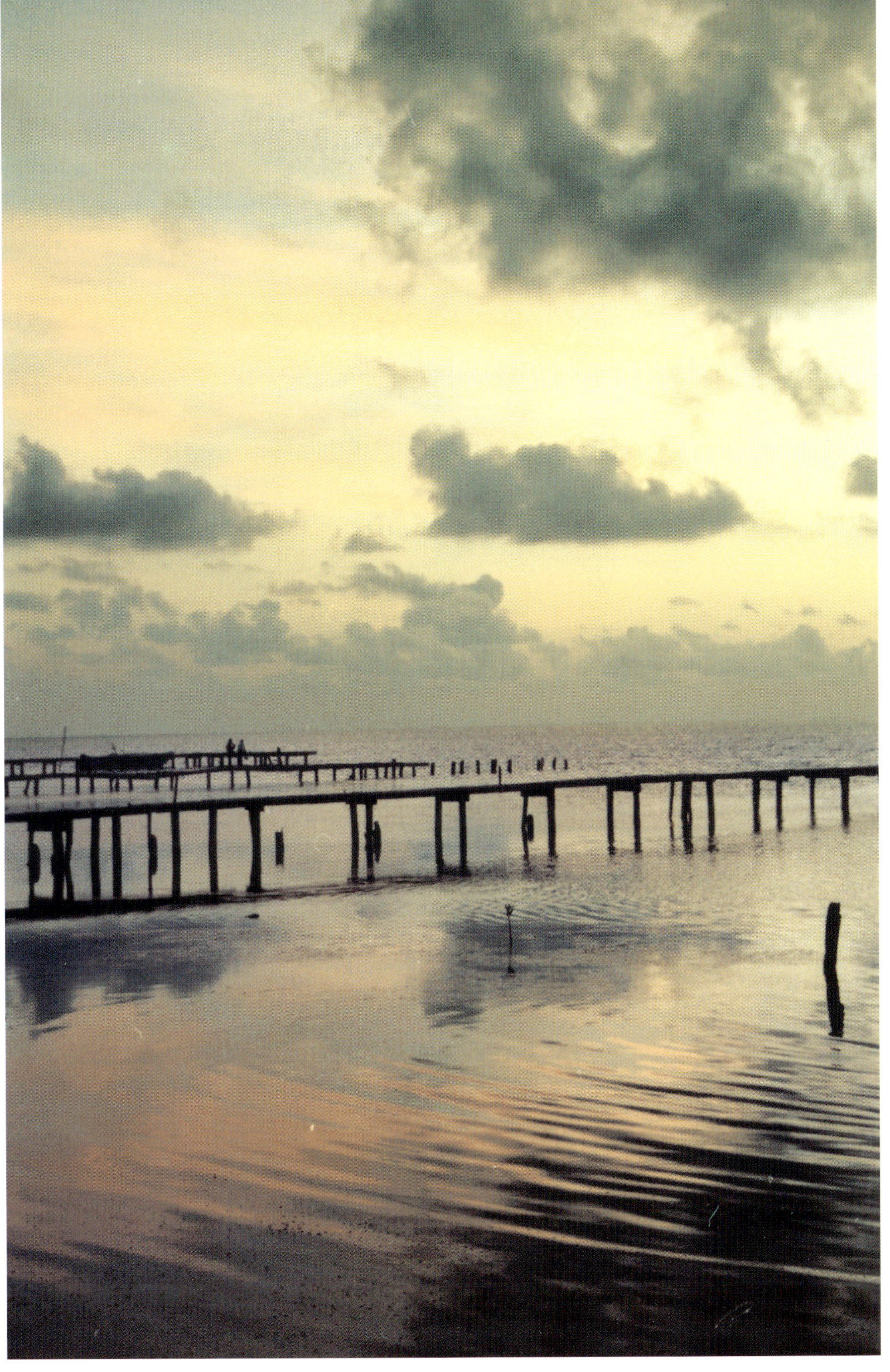

Above Trees, especially in autumn, often have photogenically strong enough shapes and colours to be pictures in their own right.
Facing page, top Overhanging branches can provide a natural frame for man-made subjects.
Facing page, bottom Trees and their reflections are perennial favourites in photography. Avoid hackneyed images by varying the height of the camera above the water.

Lines and shapes Slopes and curves are often the keys to a successful landscape. A road or a river meandering across a landscape can add interest to a picture by creating lines which draw the viewer's eye into the shot. These lines work best when leading the eye to a particular object. In addition to providing the viewer with a sense of scale, they put the scene into context. Although lines can lead to a focal point, they should generally not bisect it. Try to move the camera so that, say, a tree sits on the horizon rather than being half below it, half above it, which can look rather awkward.

Crops and trees When composing a scene, try thinking in terms of blocks of colour – like the ever-popular tulip and rape fields shot against blue skies. Many crops make appealing subjects due to their uniformity of colour and regularity of layout. Grain crops just prior to harvest, for example, possess a beautiful golden colour which will contrast with a bright sky, and can be emphasized with raking light from the side.

Trees are photogenic at all times of year, particularly when bedecked with their autumnal colours – shoot them either as part of a larger landscape or as subjects in themselves.

What is in the frame? Probably the easiest method of manipulating detail in the picture is to choose the right lens. When dealing with the monumental scale of, say, the Grand Canyon, focusing solely on a section of cliff will rob the scene of all its grandeur.

Provided there is an object of known size in the

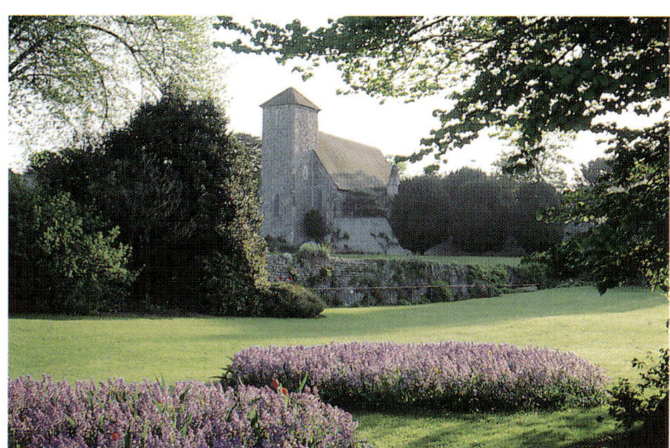

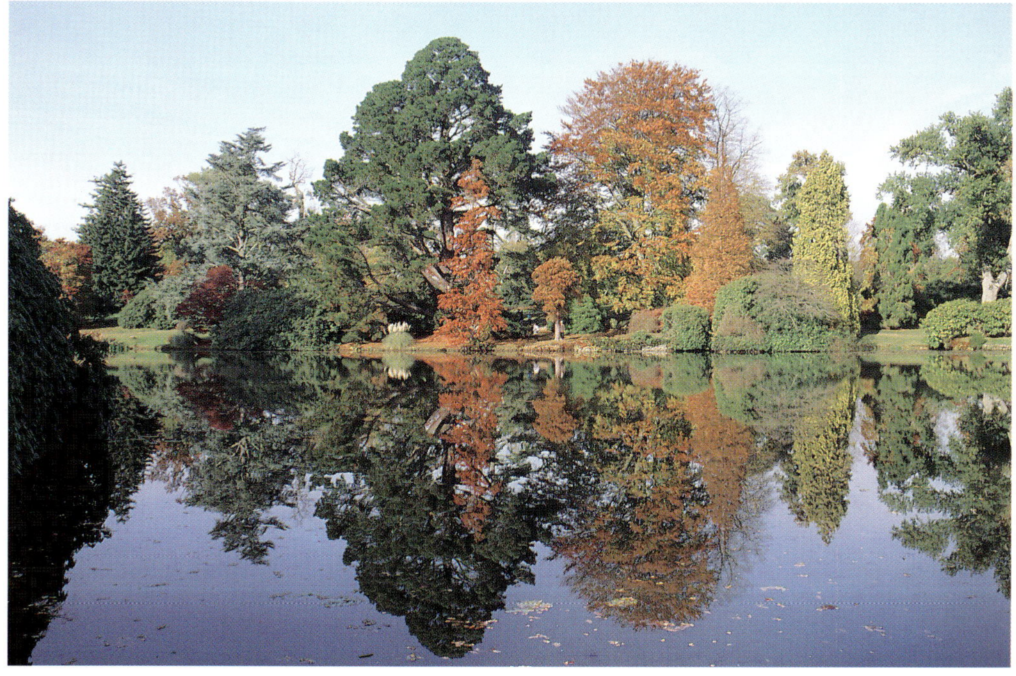

Below An alternative to the traditional sweeping vista landscape is to frame tightly around a near subject.

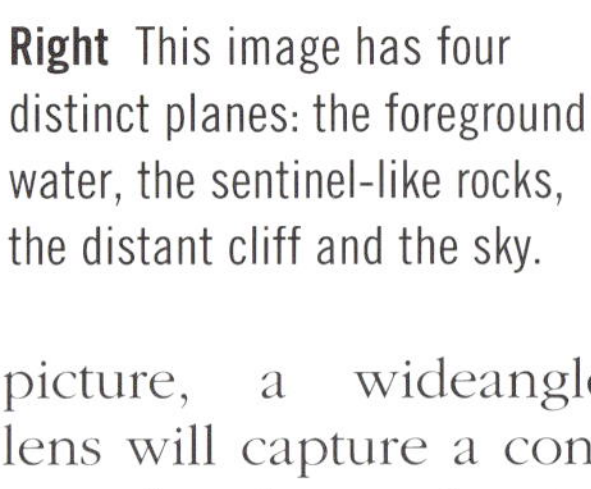

Right This image has four distinct planes: the foreground water, the sentinel-like rocks, the distant cliff and the sky.

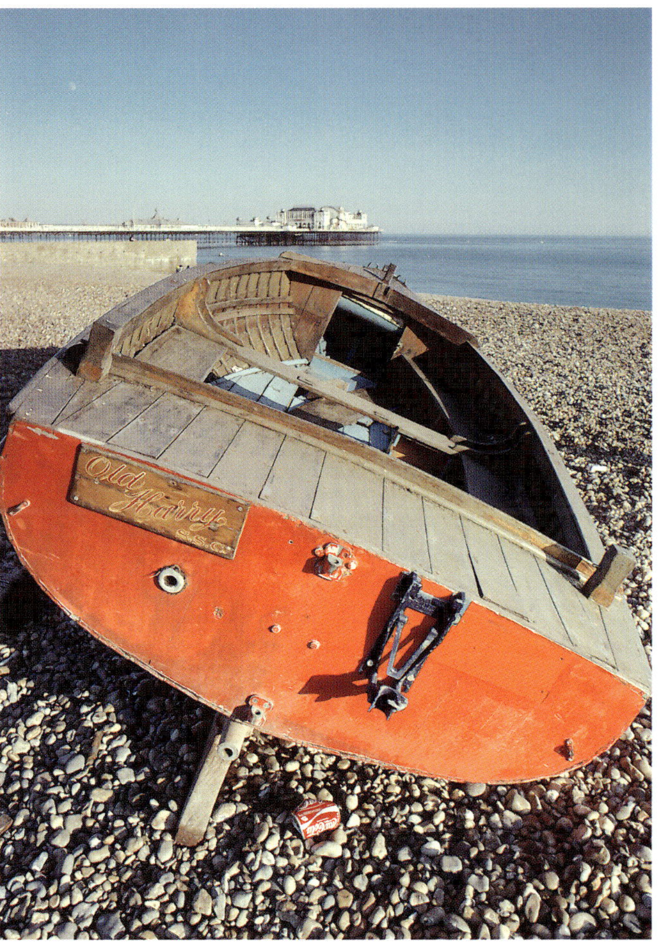

picture, a wideangle lens will capture a contrast in size and reinforce the enormity of the main subject. An alternative approach is to put an object close to the camera so that it almost fills the frame while the background peeps through.

You do not need to include the whole of the landscape in frame, and sometimes focusing on a particular subject in the foreground will create more impact.

Planes Think of the place where each subject in a scene is located as being a vertical plane. A combination of camera position and focal length lets you manipulate the distance these planes look to be apart. Getting close to the nearest plane will make the others look far away and, with a wideangle lens, smaller than is truly the case. Moving further away from the nearest item of interest while using a telephoto will make the planes look closer together and the nearer subject seem a similar size to the background.

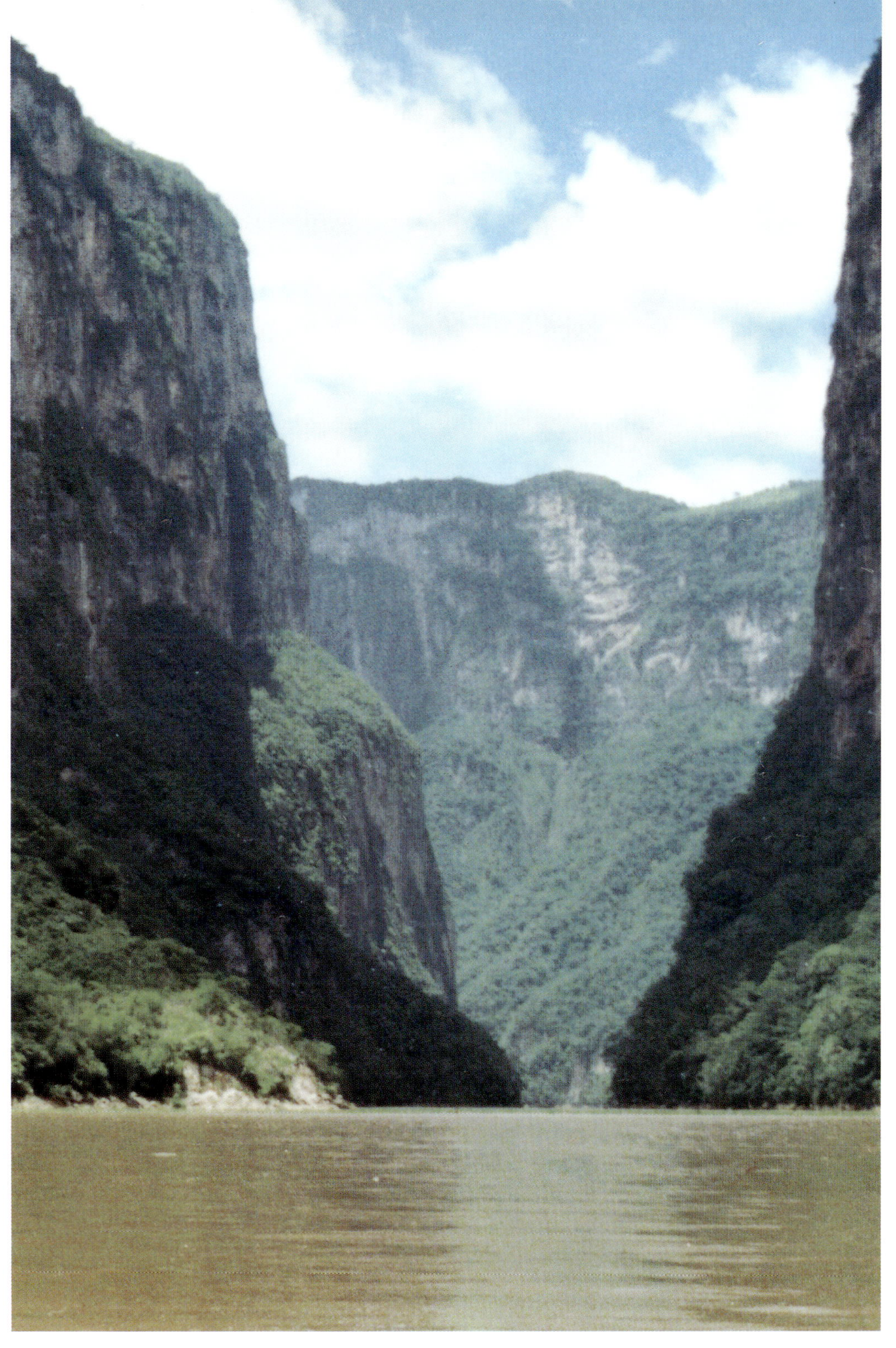

Subject Movement

Unless you are undertaking a still life or an extremely tranquil landscape, at some point you need to face the problem of dealing with subject movement. A moving subject can be treated in one of three ways: by freezing the subject and background; by blurring the subject in front of a static background; or by freezing the subject in front of a moving background.

The ability of a camera to freeze the movement of a subject is dependent on five factors:

- the speed of the subject;
- the shutter speed set on the camera;
- the distance of the subject at the moment of exposure;
- the focal length of the lens in use;
- the direction of movement of the subject.

Looking at the charts shown in this chapter, you can see how the first four factors affect the choice

ACTION-FREEZING SHUTTER SPEEDS

Subject distance (metres)	28mm lens				50mm lens			
	Subject speed (mph)							
	5	10	25	50	5	10	25	50
5	1/350	1/750	1/2000	1/4000	1/750	1/1500	1/4000	1/8000
10	1/180	1/350	1/1000	1/2000	1/350	1/750	1/2000	1/4000
15	1/125	1/250	1/750	1/1500	1/250	1/500	1/1500	1/3000
20	1/90	1/180	1/500	1/1000	1/180	1/350	1/1000	1/2000
30	1/60	1/125	1/350	1/750	1/125	1/250	1/750	1/1500
50	1/45	1/90	1/1890	1/350	1/90	1/125	1/350	1/750

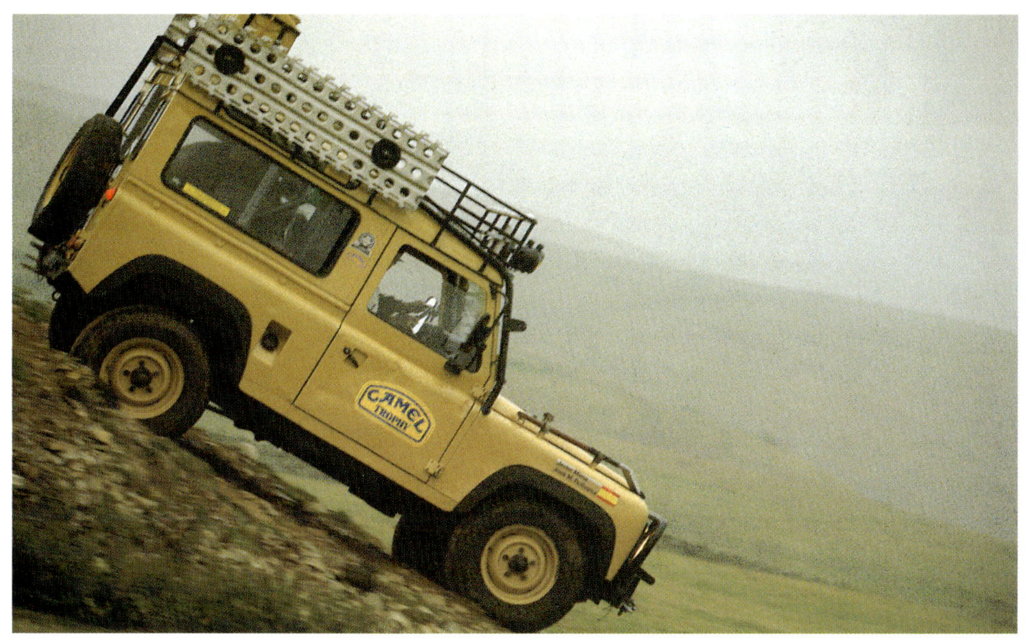

Above Action can be implied by the angle of the subject as well as its movement.

of the shutter speed. The figures assume that the pictures will be taken on medium-speed film and viewed on 10 x 8in prints at arm's length. If the film you use has a finer grain or the prints will be larger or viewed nearer, you need to use a faster

	135mm lens				300mm lens			
	5	10	25	50	5	10	25	50
	1/2000	1/4000	1/10000	N/A	1/4000	1/8000	N/A	N/A
	1/1000	1/2000	1/6000	1/10000	1/2000	1/4000	1/10000	N/A
	1/750	1/1500	1/3000	1/6000	1/1500	1/3000	1/6000	1/12000
	1/500	1/1000	1/2000	1/4000	1/1000	1/2000	1/6000	1/10000
	1/350	1/750	1/1500	1/3000	1/750	1/1500	1/3000	1/6000
	1/180	1/350	1/1000	1/2000	1/500	1/750	1/2000	1/4000

shutter speed than indicated to ensure perfectly blur-free pictures. The charts show the shutter speeds required to freeze the movement of a subject moving across the frame. If the subject is moving at 45° to the camera, you can use a shutter speed one stop slower (such as 1/250sec instead of 1/500sec). If the subject is moving directly towards or away from the camera, a shutter speed two stops slower (for example 1/125sec instead of 1/500sec) than that shown in the charts can be used and still freeze the movement.

How much movement? The question as to just how blurred or sharp the moving parts of a scene should be is, of course, an artistic one. In the case of the three funfair pictures shown on the right, the first in the sequence used a 1/60sec shutter speed, and though it is not completely frozen, it does not really give the impression of movement. The second shot, which was taken at 1/4sec, gives a great impression of speed, but there is no human element to the pictures. The final shot (taken at an intermediate shutter speed of 1/15sec) shows both the movement of the wheel and the identifiable human forms that give the picture scale as well as interest.

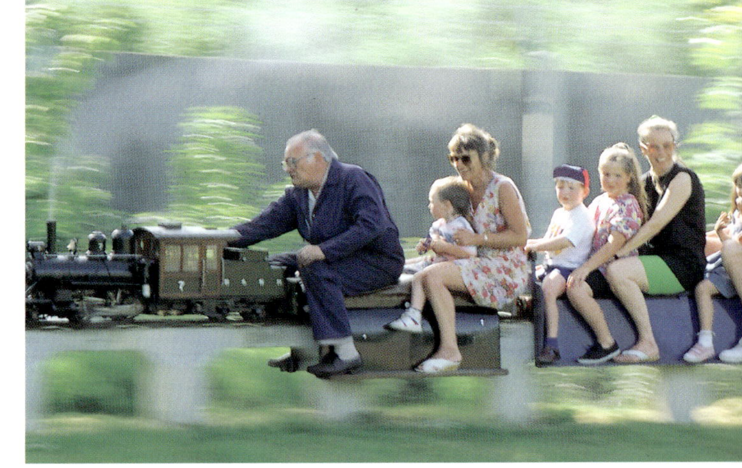

Movement within movement When you look at a person running, you tend to be conscious of their horizontal speed, but not always of the movement of their arms and legs. By setting a shutter speed that will freeze the horizontal travel of the runner,

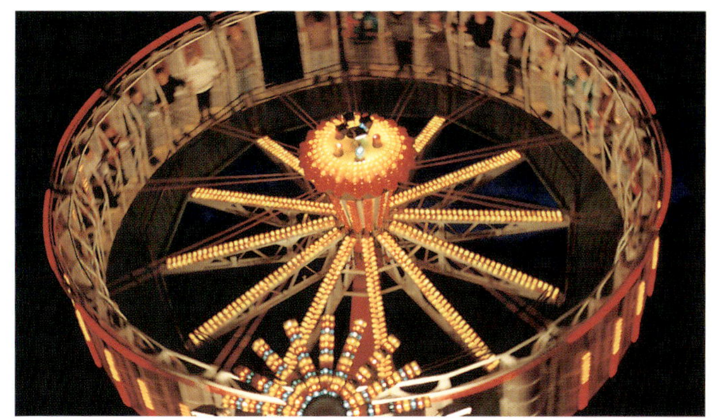

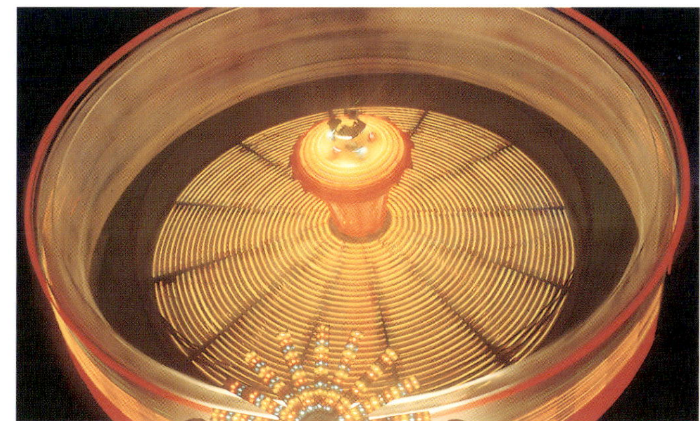

Right, top to bottom
Choosing the right shutter speed to emphasize movement is not always easy. The first shot uses too short a shutter speed while the second is too blurred. The final shot shows movement and keeps detail.
Left Following a subject's movement during exposure allows it to remain sharp while its background is blurred.

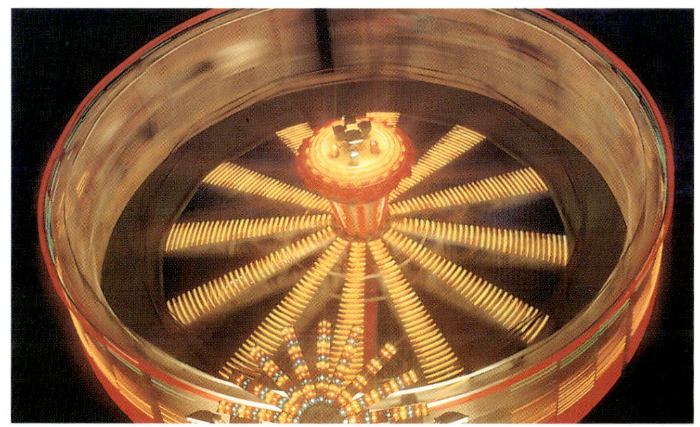

it will still show the arms and legs as slightly blurred – reinforcing the impression of movement. Successfully capturing movement on a still camera often relies on this compromise of sharp and blurred elements to the picture.

Panning Probably the best-known way of keeping part of the subject sharp while the rest flashes past in a blur of speed is panning. This is a technique that involves following a moving subject with the camera during exposure.

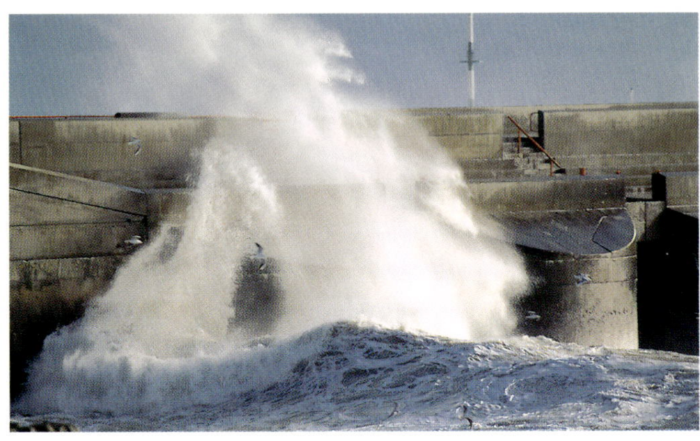

With a 35mm SLR, the viewfinder is dark during exposure, so it is necessary to practise panning. To ensure that you are tracking the subject at the correct speed, it is worth panning with the subject before the shutter is pressed, and (rather like with a golf swing) to follow through after the shutter has closed.

Above Freezing the crashing of a wave slows the awesome power of the sea.
Right A blurred shot of moving water conveys a softer, more pastoral feeling.

The photographer can also control the amount of blurring in the background. By using a longer shutter speed or a longer focal length lens, the amount of background blur will be greatly increased. It is possible to overdo it, though. If the pan is too long in, say, the case of a car passing parallel to the camera, the distance of the car relative to the camera will change during the exposure so parts of the car will not be sharp.

No smoke without movement With man-made or even man-performed movement, smoke can be a powerful visual clue to movement. The obvious example of this is steam trains. Because we are all familiar with the movement of these beasts, and the movement of smoke with wind, a trail of smoke lets the viewer know that the subject at the front of it is moving quickly.

Moving elements Of course, it is not only man-made things that move. In addition to the obvious moving subjects like animals and insects, it is possible to capture the movement of the skies and the seas by using longer exposures. It may seem ironic, but in the case of the sea's movements, the more dramatic the sea, the less blur is needed to capture a real impression of its power.

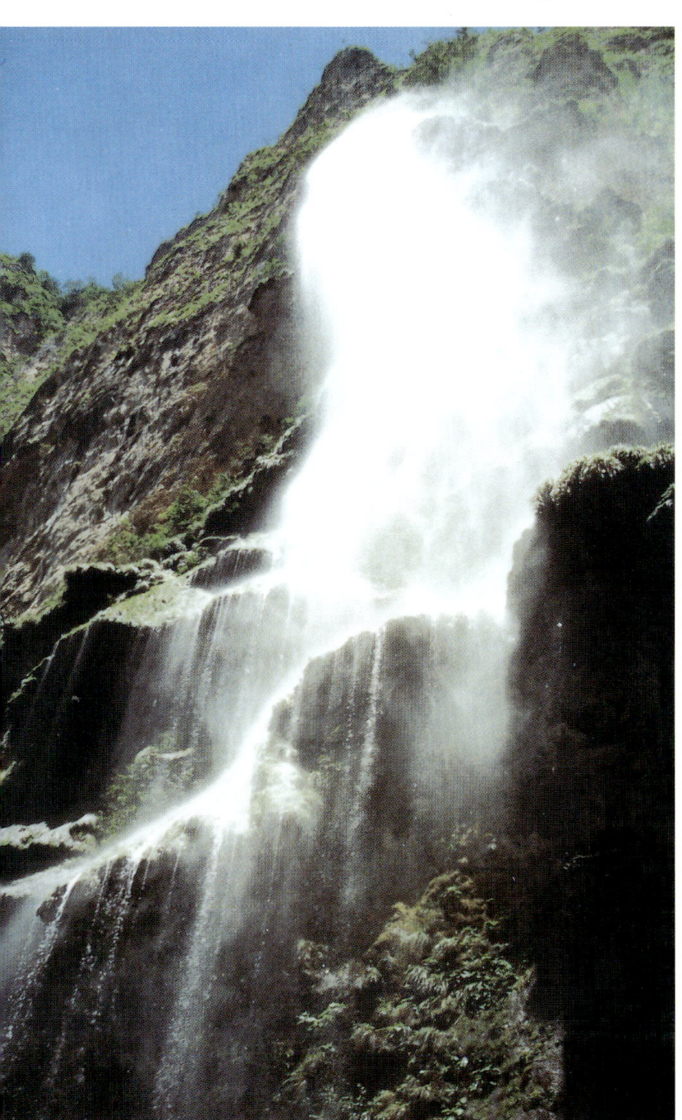

With a really stormy sea, only a very fast shutter speed will do it justice, as the spray from waves which crash on rocks will be suspended in mid-air for only a fraction of a second. To get a subtler effect, gentler seas can be exposed for relatively long periods. Taken to the extreme, this will give even a rough sea a milky or misty effect with no discernible wave. On a less extreme scale – say an exposure of a couple of seconds – it is possible to keep the shape of waves, but to soften them and imbue them with an obvious element of movement.

Processing

There is a temptation to think that once the shutter has been pressed and the picture taken, it is the end of the photographic process. Nothing could be further from the truth. Developing your own film and finally making your own prints allows you to add a great degree of creative manipulation to the photographic process.

Why use developers? When light hits a film it causes the formation of silver atoms from the ionic silver lattice. That is, an image registers on the film. If this image were fixed it would not be visible to the naked eye, and is therefore known as the latent (or hidden) image. The hidden image needs to be amplified so that it is visible, and this is achieved chemically by using a developer. The difference development makes to an emulsion is to increase the sensitivity one thousand million times – the difference between an exposure of 1/1000sec at f/8 and 15 days at f/8.

Monochrome developer ingredients The latent image tends to be formed on the surface of the crystal (or grain), and the job of the developing agent for monochrome films is to turn these exposed grains of silver halide into black metallic silver. But the developing agent is just one of a number of ingredients that a developer needs to do this. In order to leave the unexposed silver halides as they are, a restrained agent is also needed. Also, a developer is likely to contain a preservative to prevent the solution being oxidized by contact with the air. Finally there is an alkali (or accelerator) which creates the right chemical environment for the developing agent to work in. In some developers, the accelerator is contained in a separate solution to allow far greater control over contrast when uprating films. These ingredients are usually found either as a powder or as a made-up stock solution with water.

Loading the film spiral

1 Before loading the film into the tank, the end of it may need to be retrieved from the film canister,

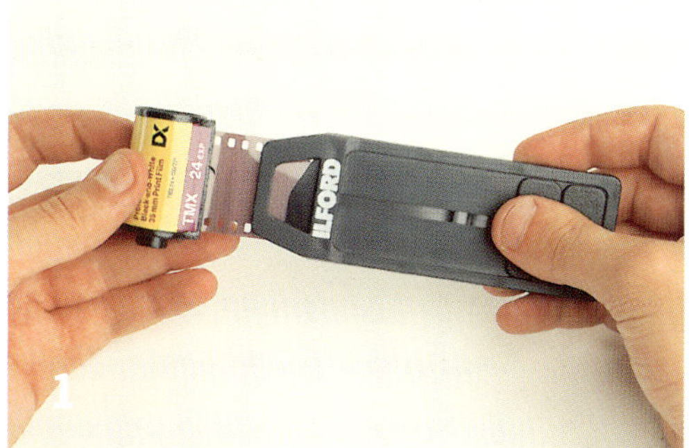

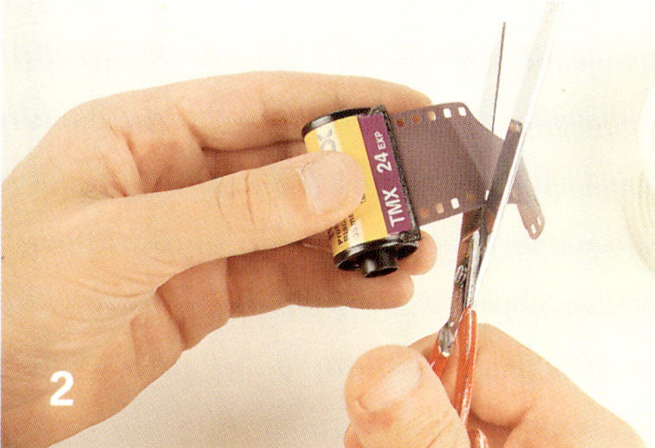

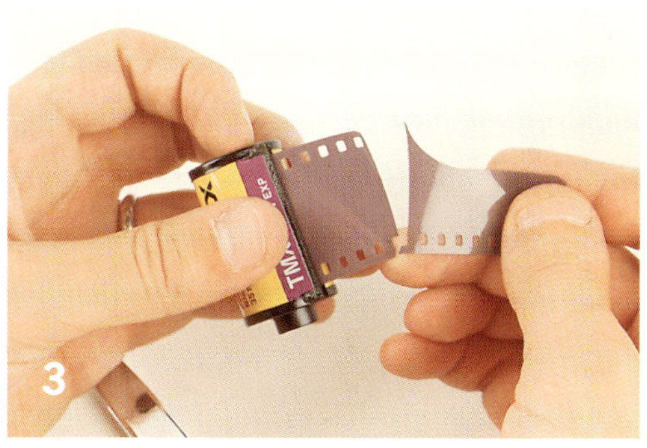

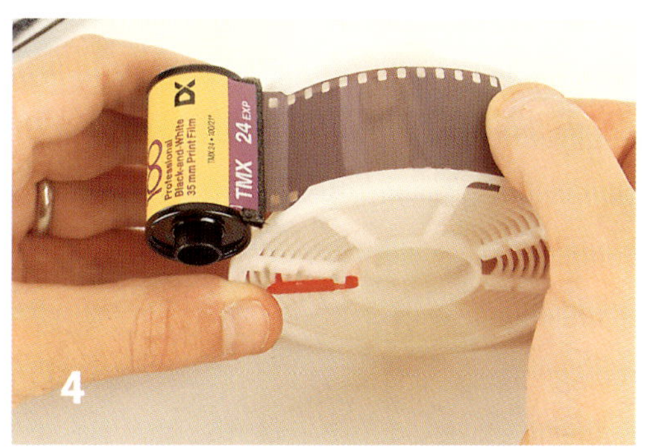

using a specially designed gadget (available from photographic suppliers).

2 Once the leader has been retrieved, the end of the film needs to be trimmed so it can be fed onto the film spiral. Cut flat across the film just behind the leader.

3 Round off the edges to leave ready for loading.

4 Present the trimmed film just past the ball-bearings on the spiral.

All the steps so far can be carried out in daylight, but now the lights must be turned off and the room must be entirely free of light.

5 Pull the film canister until about a foot or so of film is between the spiral and the canister. With the left hand still, rotate the right hand clockwise (when viewed from the back of the hand) as far as it will go, then rotate it anti-clockwise then clockwise and so on until the film canister has nearly reached the spiral. Pull the canister back to reveal more film then repeat the clockwise-anti-clockwise rotations. Repeat the operation until you pull the canister and no more film comes out.

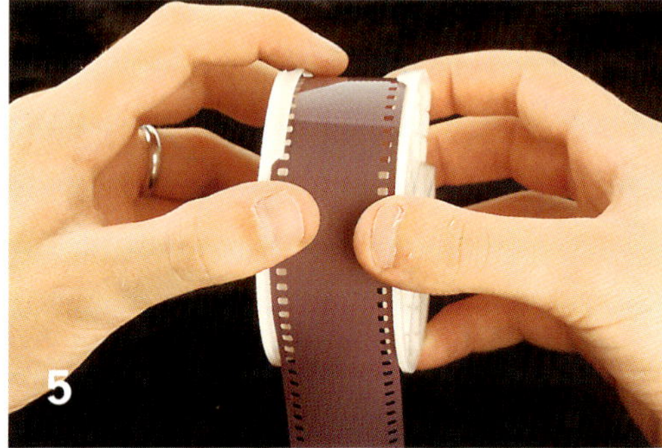
5

6 Locate the canister, and cut the film just before it.

7 Put the spiral into the developing tank.

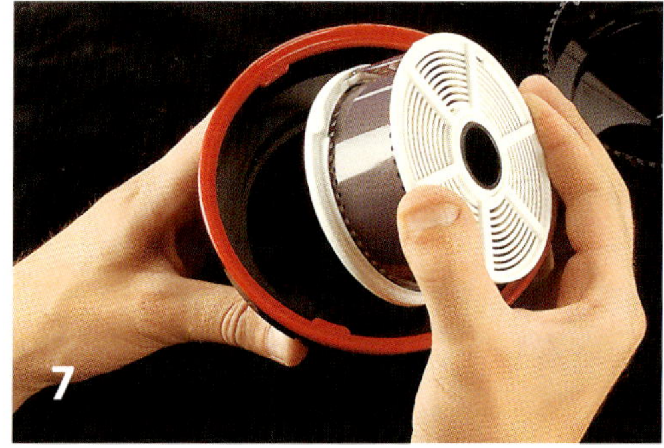
7

8 Lock on the lightproof funnel.

The lights can now be switched on again.

Once the film has been loaded, the chemicals should be mixed and heated according to the processs involved and the type of chemicals being used.

Mono print film processing This is the simplest of the film processes in terms of the chemicals involved and the temperature required for processing (normally room temperature). There is a minimal amount of equipment required in addition to a darkroom and the chemicals required for the particular process. All you need is a couple of measuring cylinders, a developing tank and a supply of water at the correct temperature.

• Put the developing chemicals into the tank through the funnel and start the clock.

• Agitate as per developing instructions. (See panel on next page.)

• Drain the developer out of the tank and pour in the stop bath, then invert the tank so as to remove any air bubbles from the film. As the developing agent needs an alkaline environment in which to function, pouring in an acidic stop bath (normally a weak solution of acetic acid) will instantaneously neutralize it. Stop baths can be reused and often contain an indicator solution which changes colour as the acid is neutralized by the alkali of the developer.

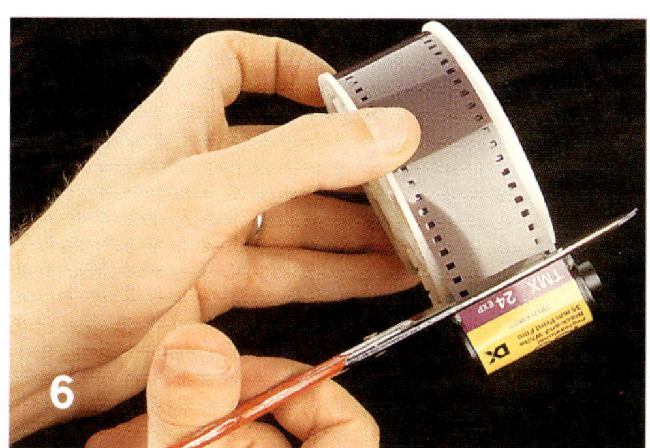

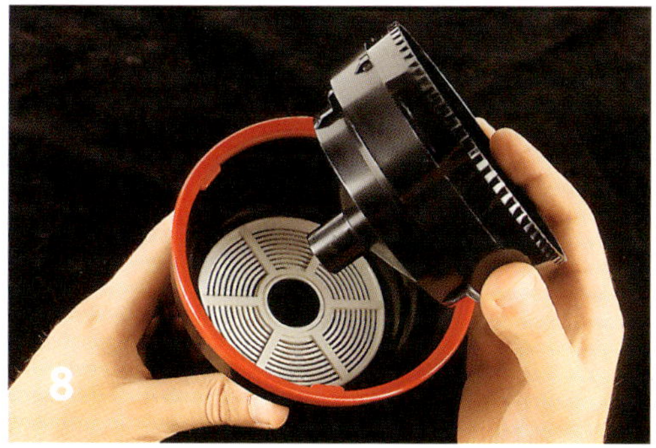

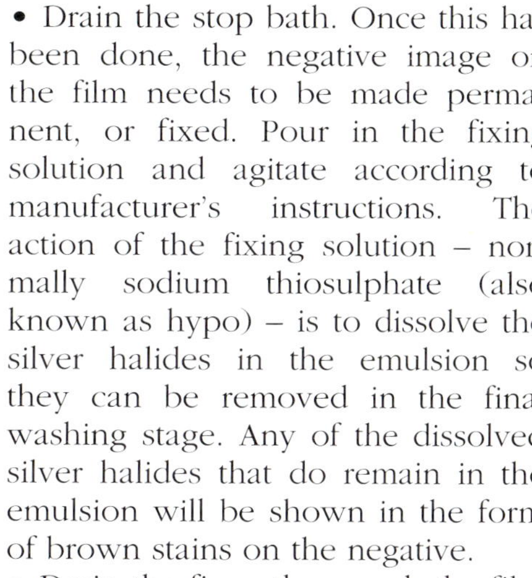

• Drain the stop bath. Once this has been done, the negative image on the film needs to be made permanent, or fixed. Pour in the fixing solution and agitate according to manufacturer's instructions. The action of the fixing solution – normally sodium thiosulphate (also known as hypo) – is to dissolve the silver halides in the emulsion so they can be removed in the final washing stage. Any of the dissolved silver halides that do remain in the emulsion will be shown in the form of brown stains on the negative.

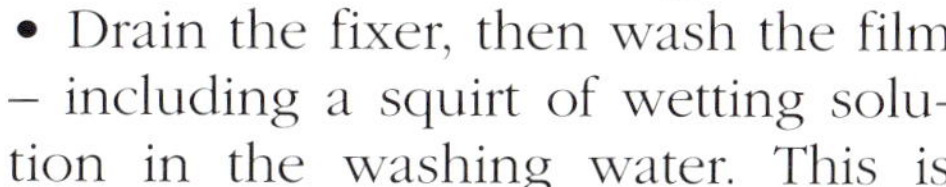

• Drain the fixer, then wash the film – including a squirt of wetting solution in the washing water. This is simply an efficient detergent that allows water to flow off the film more easily.

• Some darkroomers like to squeegee their films softly to remove excess water at this point, but it is essential that the rubber blades should be kept scrupulously clean and free of grit, or there is a risk that scratches may result on the film.

• The film should then be dried in an area that is as dust-free as possible.

Agitation If chemicals were simply splashed over the film in the spiral, it is fairly obvious that the film would not receive even development or fixing. Just pouring the chemicals into the tank and leaving them in contact with the film will not give even development either. So it is necessary to agitate the tank to make sure that no air pockets form on the film, preventing access to the developer. There are two main methods of agitation: rotating the spiral with a special key through the funnel, or by the inversion method.

The latter is more effective, and, as its name suggests, involves upending the development tank so that exhausted developer runs off the film as it is mixed around. The tank needs to have a waterproof lid attached before this is done (see first picture).

To ensure that further air bubbles are not caused by excessive shaking, the action should be a smooth inversion and then back to upright (see pictures, right). The amount of agitation required for a particular process should be detailed in the processing instructions accompanying the chemicals.

With colour developing, the tank should be placed back in the water bath after each agitation to keep the chemicals inside at the correct temperature.

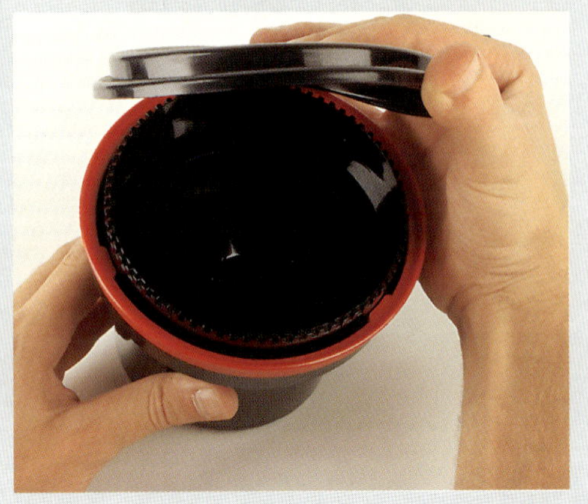

OTHER PROCESSES

Colour negative and transparency films are processed along similar lines, but with different chemicals, temperatures and timings. It is worth looking at how the processes differ.

Colour negative processing Colour negative films need to record the colour as well as the presence of light and have three layers of silver halide, each geared to a different primary colour. Coupled to each of these layers is a colour former: cyan for the red sensitive layer, yellow for the blue layer and magenta for the green layer. When the developing

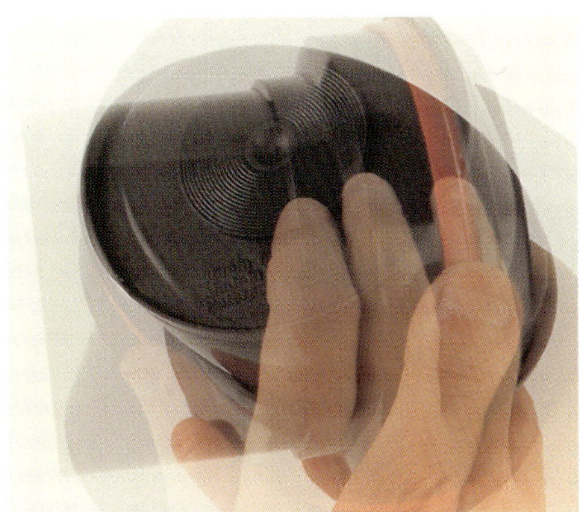

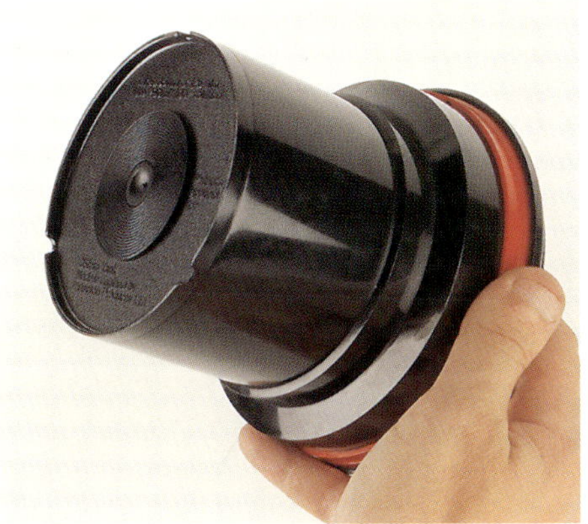

agent comes into contact with the exposed silver halides it reacts to form metallic silver. But the key reaction in colour negative processing is between the oxidized developer and the colour former. The product of this reaction is a dye of the (almost) opposite colour and density to the light that fell on the film.

The bleach/fix (also known as BLIX) stage removes the metallic silver and the residual silver halides from the emulsion. The film should then be washed and dried as per monochrome films.

Caution: colour chemicals should be treated with care as they can be toxic.

Colour slide developing First the film is developed to get a negative mono image in the three layers. The film is then reversed (fogged) chemically. In effect, what happens is that only those areas of the three emulsions that were not exposed to light are affected – the exposed grains having been turned to metallic silver. The fogging agent in a three-bath process is in the colour developer, thus the newly fogged areas are colour developed. What happens is that where, say, the film has received blue light, the blue layer has not been acted on by the colour developer, having already been turned to metallic silver in the first development. Only the green and red layers are acted on, generating colour dyes of their complements (magenta and cyan). Magenta and cyan dyes together make blue. The film at this stage is still clouded by metallic silver from the first development and silver salts from the colour development. The bleach/fix removes these, leaving only the dye image. The film is washed and dried as per the other processes.

Printing

There is a very logical school of thought that questions the point of in-camera cropping and precise exposure control if you are only going to hand the film over to someone else to print. How can a person who does not know how you saw the scene know how you want the picture printed? With black and white (monochrome) film, there is an added dimension in the form of what contrast the picture needs to be printed at. The obvious alternative is to print the picture yourself – giving you a great deal of creative control.

The darkroom Before you can go about printing, you need somewhere to do it (a darkroom), and something to do it with (an enlarger).

Right and below These three prints were made on paper of (clockwise from the top) grade 0, 4 and 2. The negative used in this case responded best to printing on grade 2 (below).

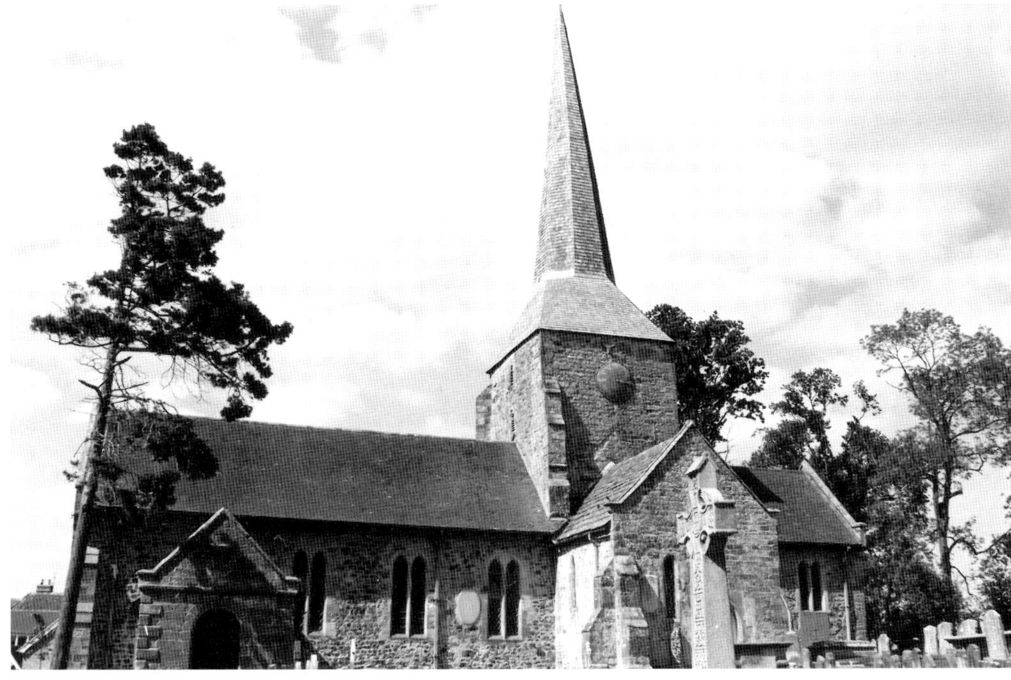

The process of printing is a mirror image of the process of exposing the picture in the first place. Much as the film needs to be prevented from coming into contact with light before or after the actual exposure, so printing paper must be prevented from being exposed to white light except during the printing exposure. Printing paper is not, however, sensitive to light of a deep amber colour. Light of this hue is said to be 'safe'. Specially designed lights for the darkroom are known as safelights, the use of which means it is possible to carry out black and white printing without being in total darkness.

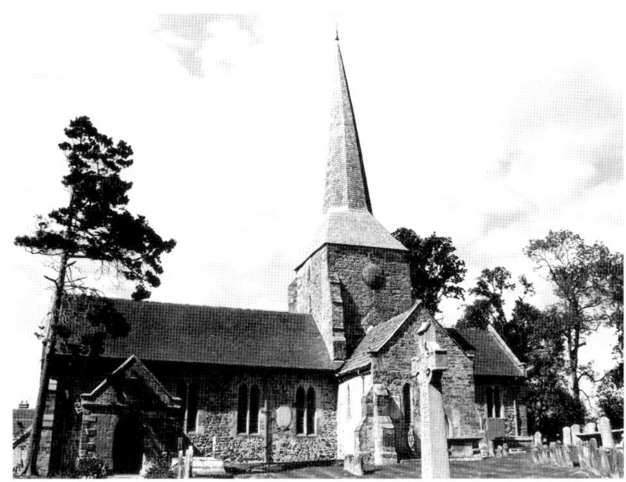

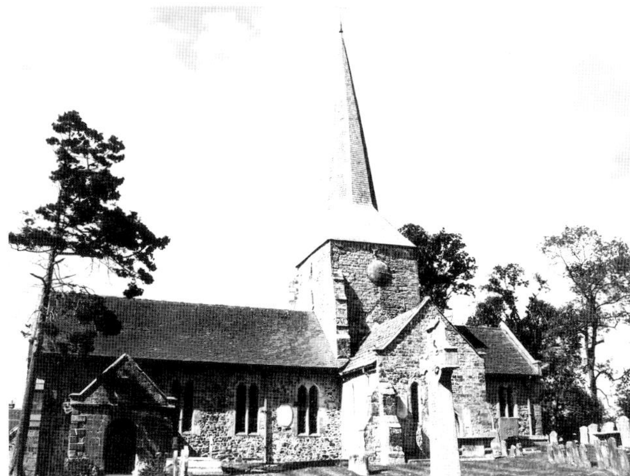

Preventing white light from entering the room is of paramount importance. Although printing paper is not 'fast' in terms of its sensitivity – about ISO 6 in film terms – the presence of any white light will cause fogging.

To be able to print, you need something that will project light from the negative onto a piece of light-sensitive paper. Obviously a print 24 x 36mm in size is no use for easy viewing, so the image needs to be enlarged. The piece of equipment you need to do this – the enlarger – has four requirements: a light source, a negative holder, a means of altering the magnification and a means of focusing the image.

To develop the print the process is the same as for developing a mono film (see pages 104–5), except that the operation can be carried out under a safelight.

Paper types and grades There are two basic types of paper: Resin Coated (RC) and Fibre Based (FB). RC paper is simpler and quicker, but purists swear by FB paper.

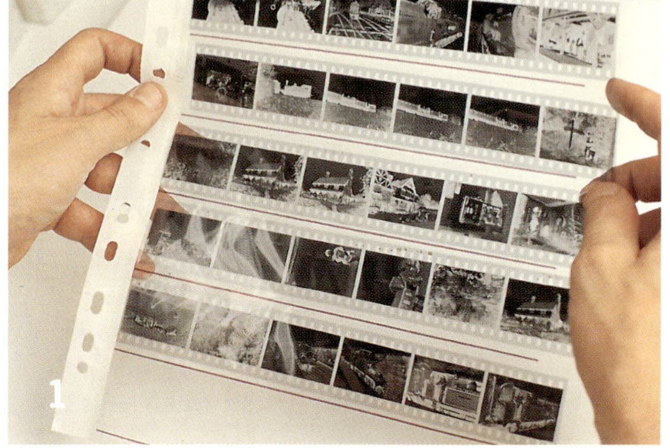
1

There is also paper of different grades of contrast available. If you have a very contrasty negative, choosing a low number grade (0 or 1) will soften the image. A negative lacking in punch would be brightened up by using a hard (high number) paper – grade 4 or 5. You can also get variable contrast paper which allows you to imitate any grade from 00 to 5. These papers work by having emulsions that are sensitive to different colours of light and, by using specially designed filters that correspond to different grades, you only have to keep one stock of paper to cover all the grades you need.

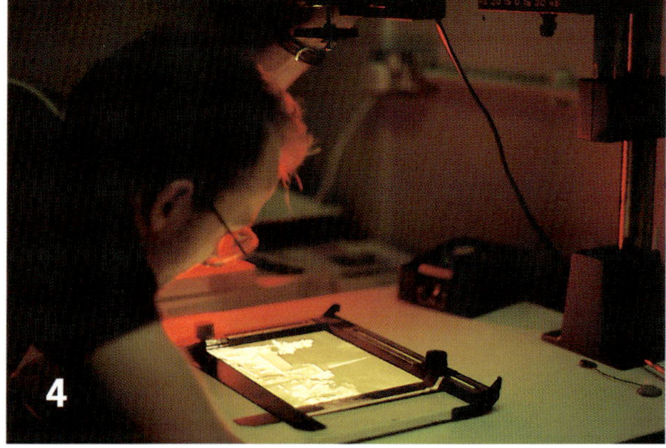
4

Making your first print

1 Pick out the negative that you want to print.

2 Check the negative for scratches, ingrained dust and stains.

3 If the neg is clear of these, remove any surface dust using either a fine brush or a blower brush.

4 Turn the lights off, turn the enlarger on and get

the magnification you desire for the print and focus at full aperture on the lens. Focus on a piece of unexposed but developed and fixed paper so the focus will be spot-on when it comes to exposing the print.

5 Turn the safelight on and place a sheet of paper under the enlarger. Push the red swing-filter

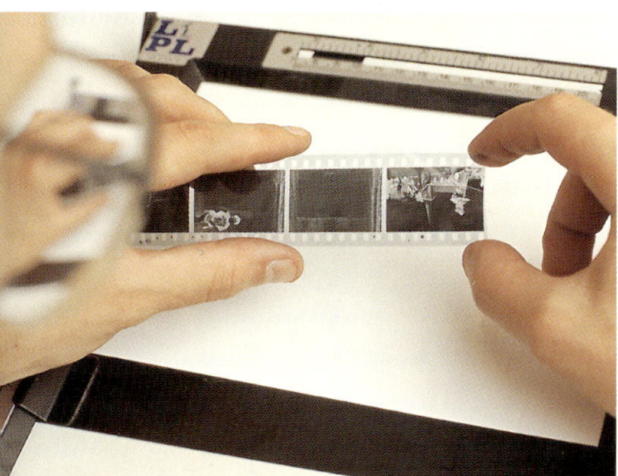

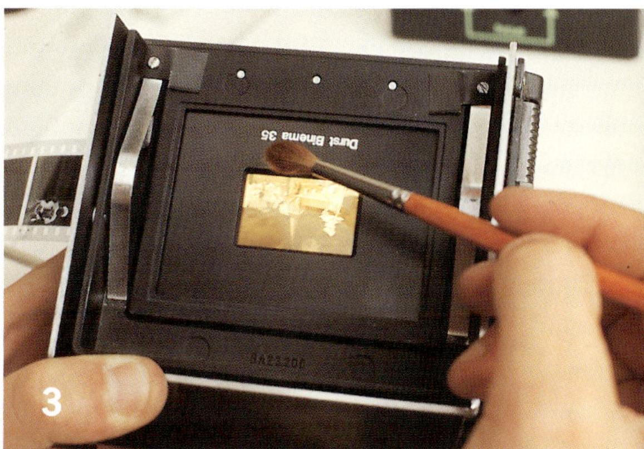

3

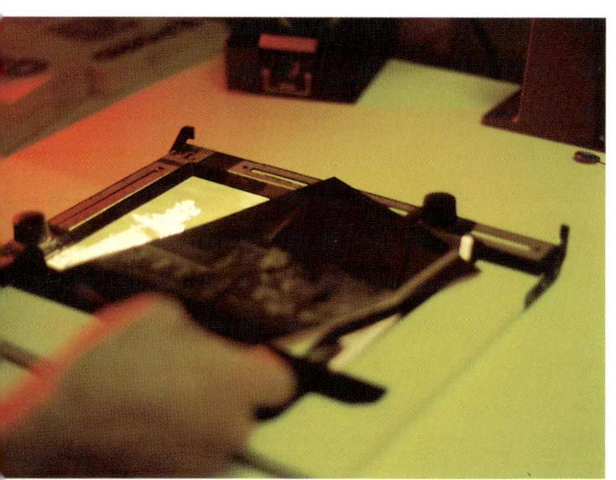

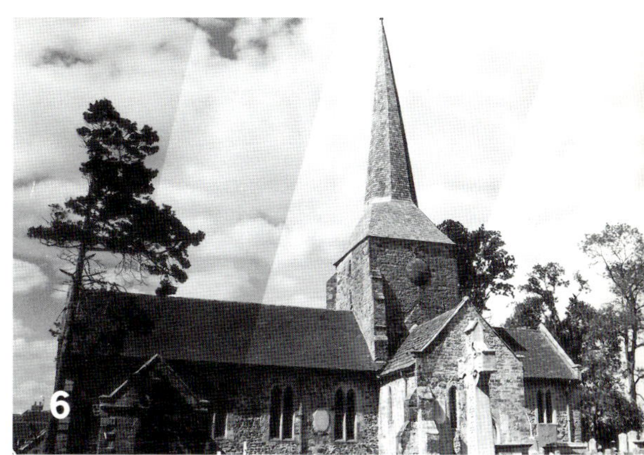

6

so it covers the lens, and check the projected image to find an angle at which a narrow strip can be placed to get a full range of tones (from white to black) at any position on the negative.

6 Stop the lens down to f/8 or f/11. Using a sheet of opaque card, expose the paper in increasing one second increments and develop and fix it (see 7&8). You should be left with a print that shows strips of increasing or decreasing density (depending on which side you started the exposure). This test strip indicated the correct exposure at around six to seven seconds to get the right tones.

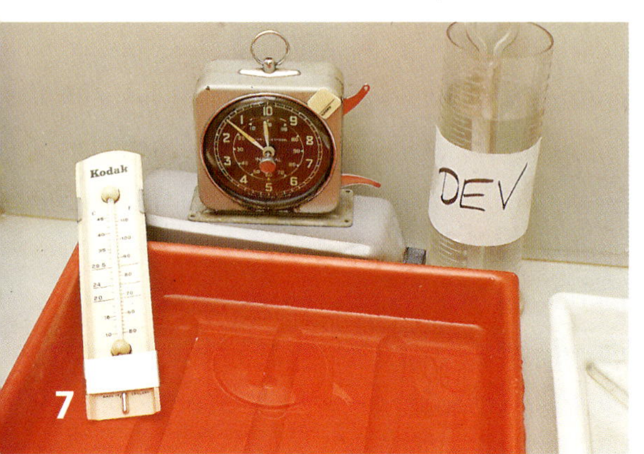

7

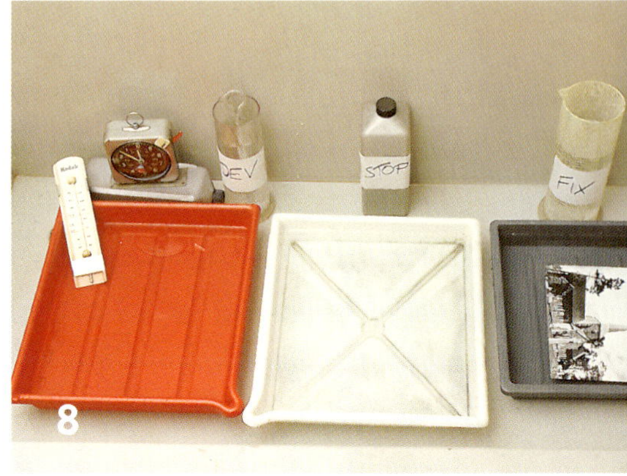

8

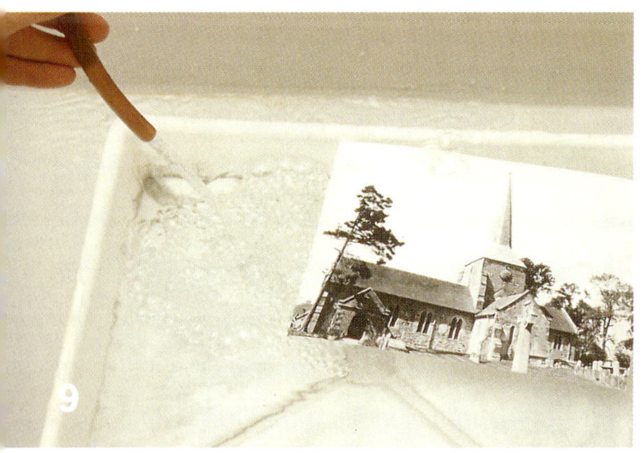
9

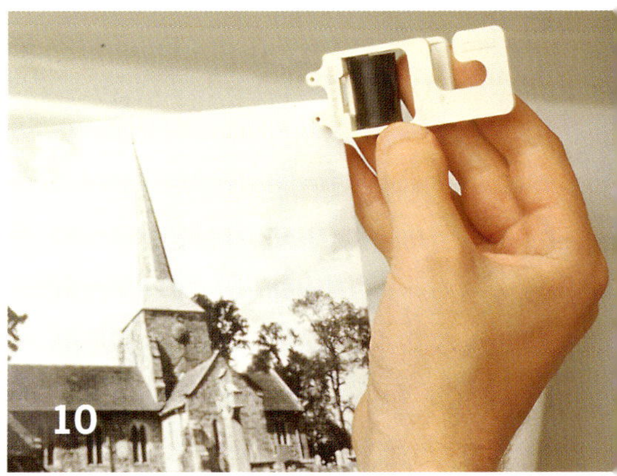
10

7&8 The dishes you use for developing, stopping the developing and fixing the image should be of different colours and always used in the same order to prevent contamination. Different measuring cylinders should also be used for developer and fixer. Develop, stop and fix as for film processing (see pages 104–5)). The processing for

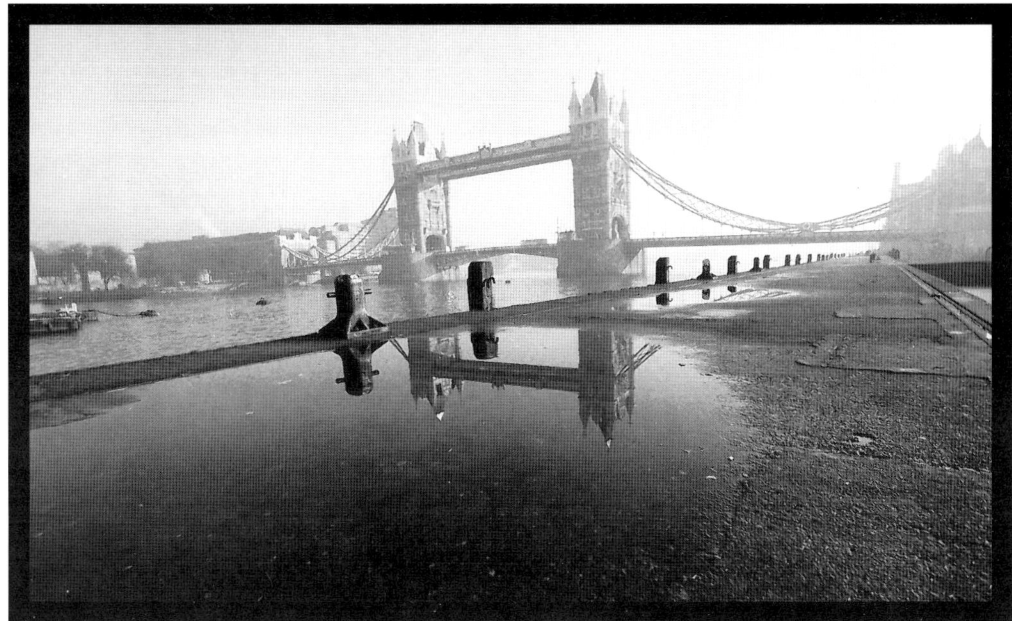

Above A straight print from the negative, on grade 2 paper, exposed for 20 seconds and framed with a black border. See next page for alternative ways of printing the same image.

black and white paper is exactly the same as for film except for two points. The size and shape of paper means that while it is possible to process it in drums, it is easier and quicker to have a separate tray (or dish) for each chemical stage. As black and white paper is not sensitive to red/orange light the process can be carried out under your inspection. Possibly the most magical moment in photography is when the image of your first print starts to appear before your eyes.

9 Once the print has been exposed for 6.5 seconds (in this example) and has been developed and fixed, it needs to be thoroughly washed.

10 After washing, the print should be left to dry in a warm – but not hot – dust-free area, hanging on a line.

When you print a black and white picture yourself, you can control four things that can make a radical difference to the look of a picture. Shots you were not sure about can be given a new

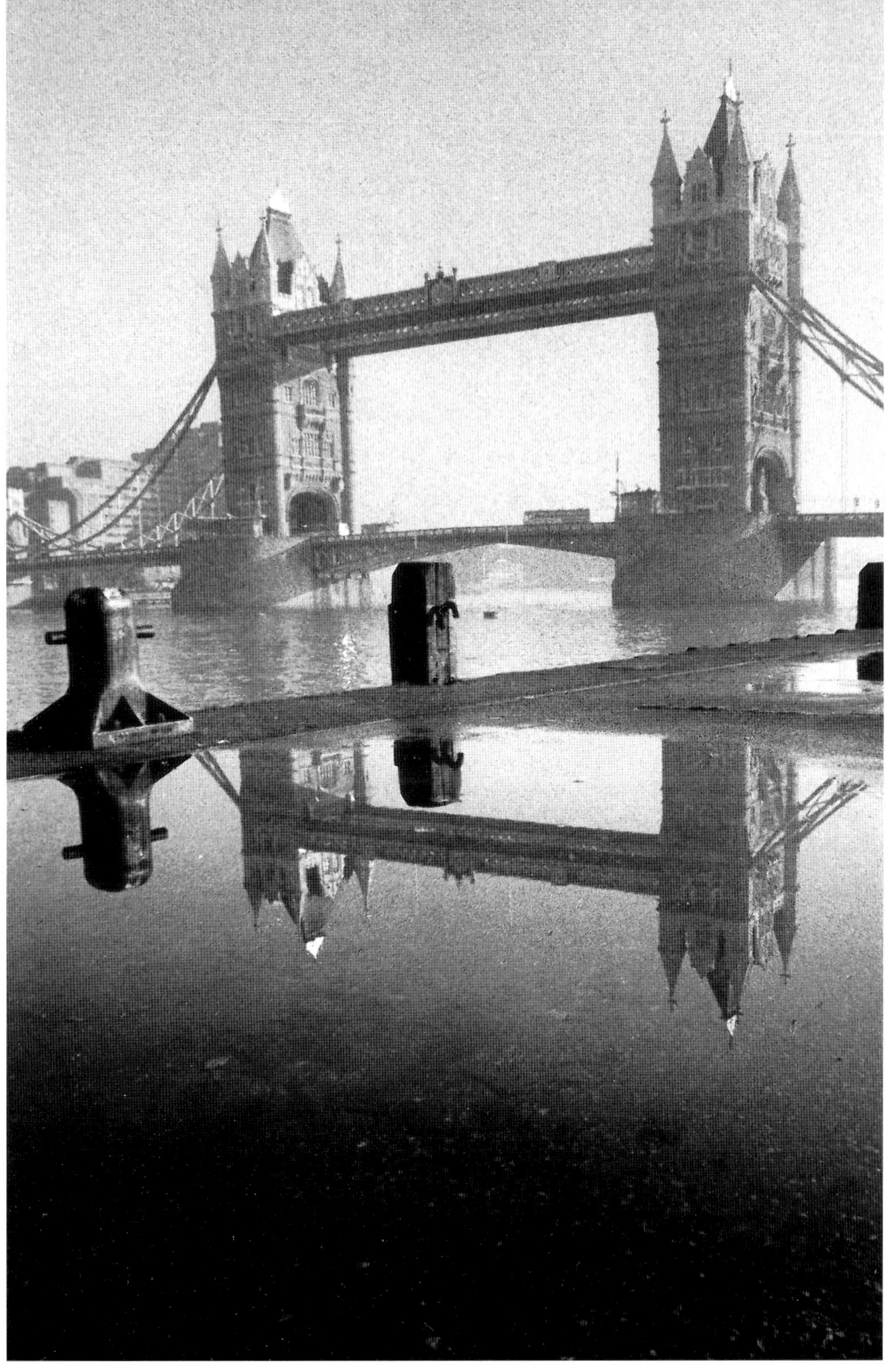

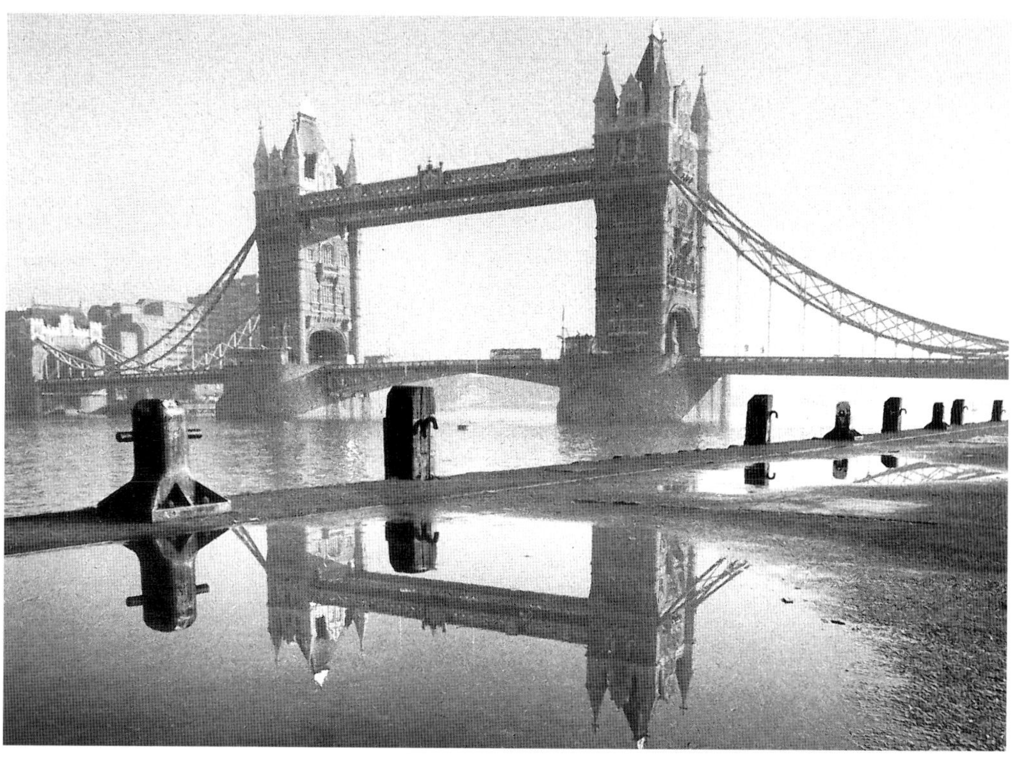

Above This was printed using the same exposure and grade of paper as the straight print (see previous page); the image has been cropped so that diagonal line leads across the page and off into infinity.

Left This also used the same exposure and paper as the straight print; the portrait format has altered the composition so as to focus attention on the centre, giving the bridge and its reflection more prominence.

angle; even apparently dull negatives can be transformed during the printing process.

By playing around with the exposure, for example, you can make clear skies seem stormy and vice versa; you can highlight one part of the picture and de-emphasize another.

With cropping, you can get rid of cluttered parts of a scene, home in on a particularly powerful image, or make an image stronger by putting leading lines coming from, rather than near, a corner.

Changing the grade of paper can alter a moody shot into a tranquil scene or achieve the reverse.

Altering the type of borders you put on a picture can radically alter its appearance. Narrow or broad, black or white, all make a difference to a scene's interpretation.

This is not a specialist printing book, but, as can be seen from the examples on these pages, it will give you a taster of how much can be achieved in the darkroom.

Other Cameras

Compacts Compact cameras are easy to use and very popular. They have a viewfinder separate from the lens and use 35mm film. For more detail see pages 119–121.

Cartridge cameras These use 110 or disc film. The forerunners of compact cameras, they are easy to use but, because of a smaller image size on the film, picture quality is not comparable to that of a cheap compact.

Medium format cameras These cameras use roll-film (known as 120 or 220) and give negative sizes of 6 x 4.5cm to 6 x 17cm depending on the camera. Some have pentaprisms, most have interchangeable lenses. They tend to be less sophisticated (electronically) than 35mm SLRs, leaving the work up to the photographer. Some have shutters in the lenses.

Large format cameras These cameras use sheet film of 5 x 4in or 10 x 8in. They tend to be used mainly for professional studio work, and many cameras allow sophisticated manipulation of depth of field and perspective.

Film size The most obvious difference between camera types is their film size. Changing the film size with which you work has three effects.

The first effect is on the amount of detail the film can record, known as its resolution. Assuming you use the same type, brand and speed of film, then the bigger the film, the more detail it can resolve. This improvement in quality is further enhanced by the fact that for both printing and projection, the degree of enlargement required to get a viewable image does not need to be as great with larger films, so grain is much less evident.

Secondly, with larger film formats, lenses need to be bigger to cover the increased film area. And the larger a lens is (in terms of diameter), the more difficult it is to manufacture to the same quality as, say, a lens for a 35mm camera. In the vast majority of cases, though, the lower absolute quality of these lenses is nowhere near enough to offset the increase in quality of the picture obtained by having a larger film.

The third effect is on the size of the camera. If a camera is going to use a larger film, it must itself be larger.

There are four basic film types in terms of size: cartridge, 35mm film, rollfilm (for medium format cameras) and sheet film (for large format cameras). Cartridge films are on the wane in photographic popularity. Where once the vast majority of point-and-shoot cameras used 126, 110 or disc cartridges, most now use 35mm film. The 126 format with a negative size of 28 x 28mm lost out

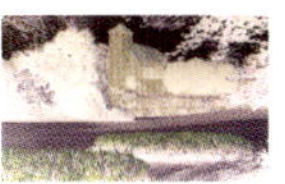

Above This is the actual size of a 110 negative.

Left Medium format cameras are mainly used for studio work, producing extremely clear results and an easily croppable 6 x 6cm image.

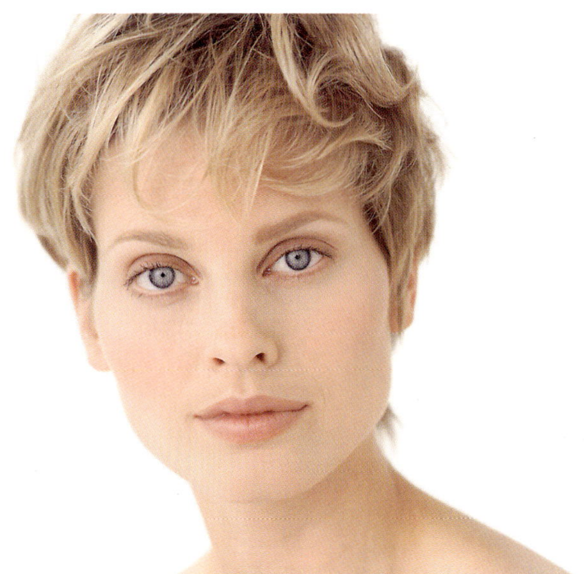

because the cameras that took it were larger than their 110 or disc replacements, and developments in film technology had made the prints from smaller formats as good as the 126 prints on older films. Subsequently, the 11 x 17mm (110) and 8 x 10mm (disc) format cameras lost out to 35mm compacts because the latter were getting small enough to pocket, and the former's negatives required so much enlargement to get a print that the quality was very poor in comparison.

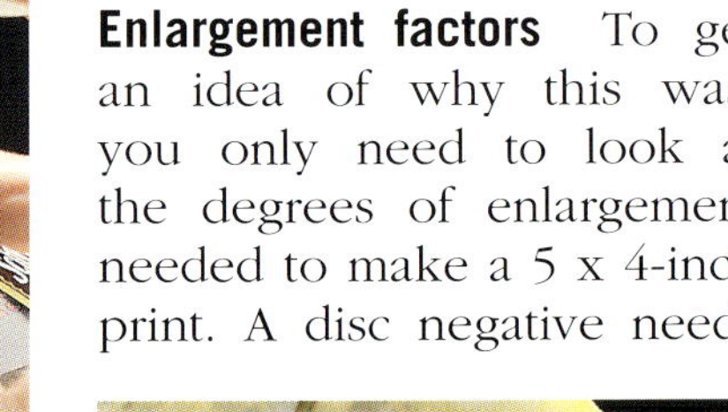

Enlargement factors To get an idea of why this was, you only need to look at the degrees of enlargement needed to make a 5 x 4-inch print. A disc negative needs a 12.7x degree of enlargement, while a 35mm format negative needs only a factor of 4.2x. These are linear enlargement factors, and if they are squared this gives the true degree of enlargement: 161x for discs and 18x for 35mm format. In other words, the print from a 35mm negative will show nine times (161 ÷ 18) as much detail as the print from a disc negative.

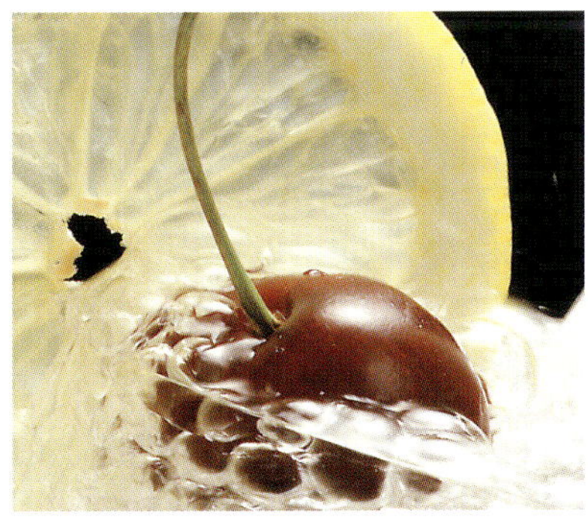

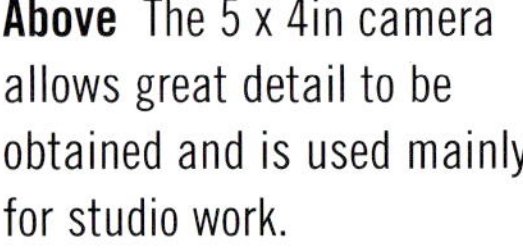

Above The 5 x 4in camera allows great detail to be obtained and is used mainly for studio work.

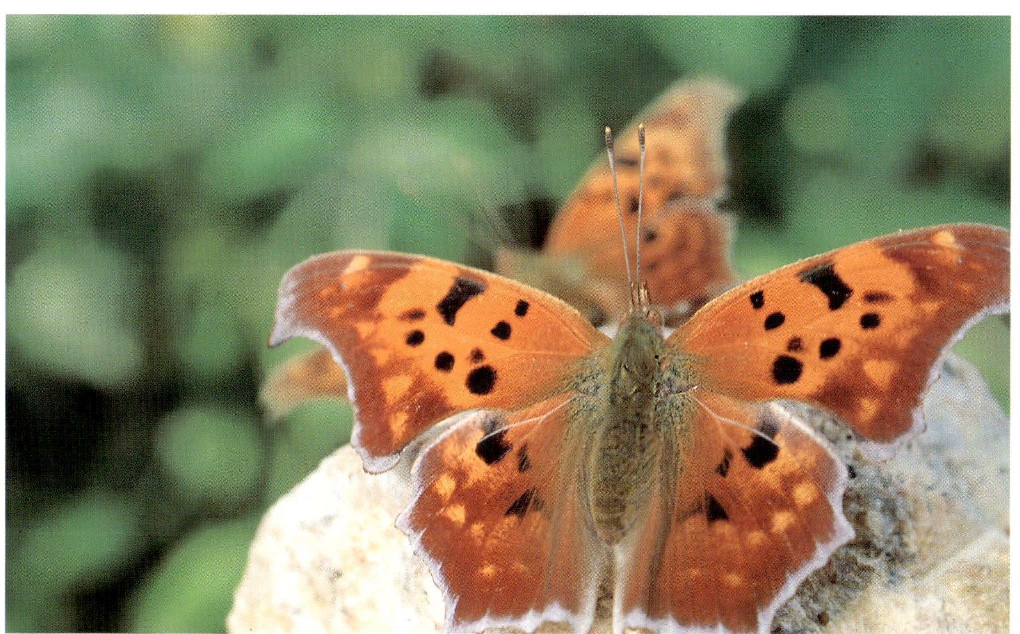

COMPACT CAMERAS

Compacts, like SLRs, use 35mm film. The significant difference between compacts and SLRs is the viewing system: compacts use direct vision viewfinders – that is, the viewfinder is separate, so that what you see is not what you get.

Parallax error When the viewing lens and the taking lens are not one and the same, they will obviously not always be looking at precisely the same scene. With distant subjects there is no problem, but if the subject is very close, large discrepancies start to arise between what is shown in the viewfinder and what appears on the film. This discrepancy is parallax error. Many direct vision viewfinders have parallax correction marks, so that when shooting within a particular distance, the photographer knows where the actual image appears within the viewed image frame.

Above When using a compact camera very close up, it is sometimes difficult to line up the subjects exactly in the viewfinder even with the parallax correction marks.

Functions Compacts are predominantly automatic cameras and as such are ideal for 'point and shoot' photography. They usually have an automatic exposure system and either autofocusing or fixed focus lenses. Most have built-in flash units and are good for grabshots or on occasions when you do not want to have the bulk of an SLR kit with you.

In recent years compact cameras have become increasingly sophisticated, adding features such as 10 shots on a single frame, multiple exposure settings, intervalometers that take a picture every minute, hour or day, and TV modes for shooting pictures off television. Many now allow some control over exposure, though not with the precision of an SLR. There is also a range of single-use cameras, including waterproof and panoramic models.

The two most useful functions to look out for are exposure compensation and focus lock. With these key features, you can exert at least some control over the creative aspects of photography.

Below By locking the focus before recomposing a picture you will avoid getting a blurred subject against a sharp background.

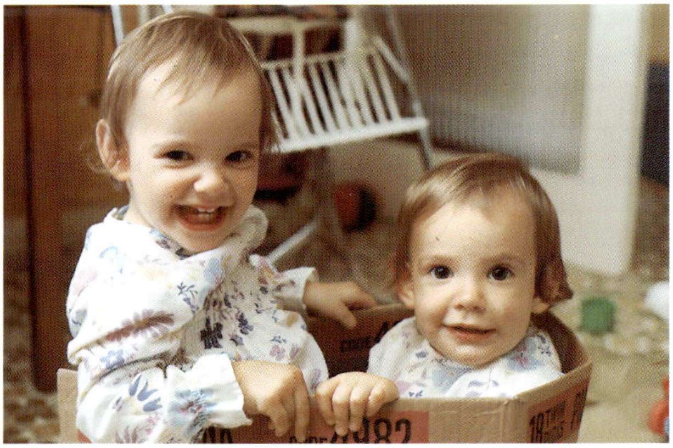

Autofocus Compacts use active autofocus systems, which work by sending out a beam of infrared light. By judging the angle at which the beam is returned it is able to calculate the distance of the object the beam has reflected off and the camera focuses the lens accordingly.

Cameras using this system have a fixed number of focusing steps. Simpler models often have few steps and rely on depth of field to cover the distances between the steps. There are innate problems with the system: as you do not view the image through the focused lens, you have no idea if the camera has got it right.

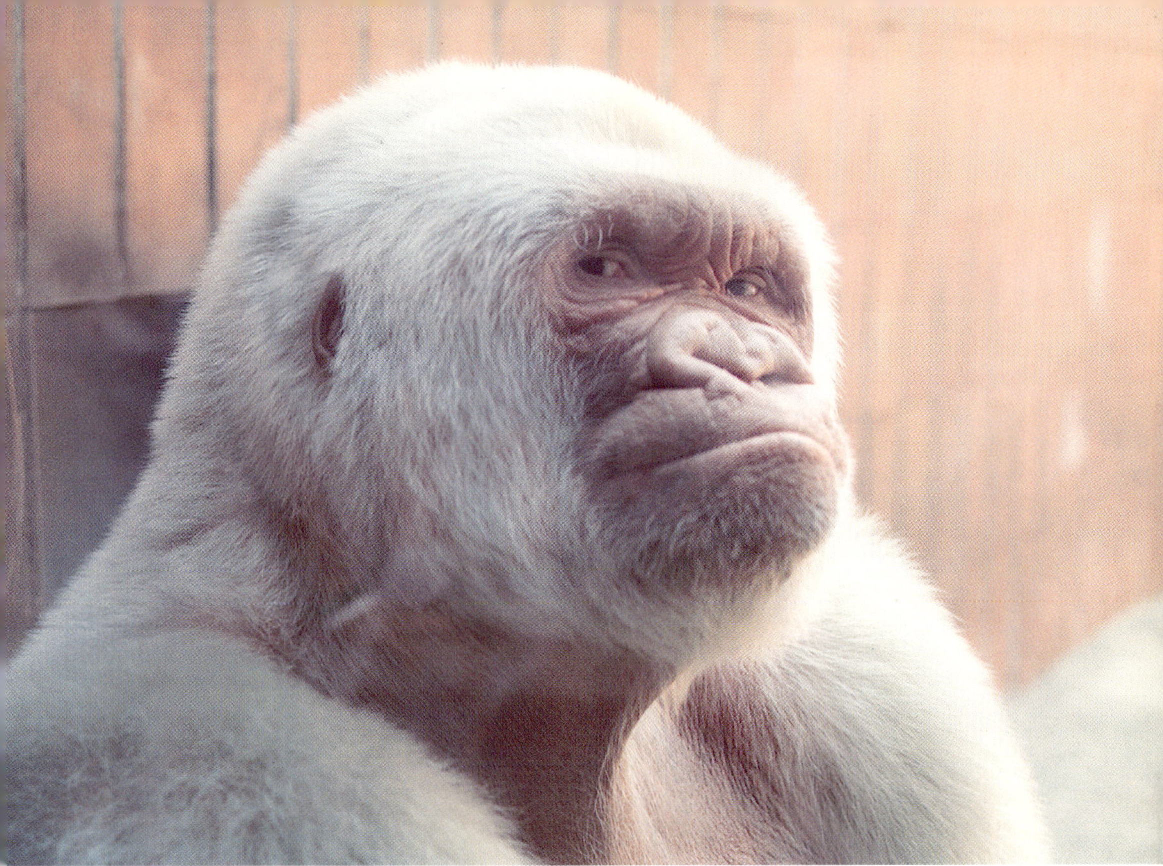

Above Using a focus lock is essential when shooting through glass if you want a sharp result.

Active systems cannot focus on a subject behind a sheet of glass. More advanced cameras have an infinity lock, which locks the focus at infinity so the camera can shoot through windows or at distant scenes. This is also useful when (as happens when the beam does not come back at all) the camera automatically focuses at the hyperfocal distance, relying on depth of field.

Film speed: controlling exposure Compacts give you little control over exposure: unlike with an SLR, you can affect neither the light coming in through the lens nor the shutter speed. The solution to the problems this can cause is to use different film speeds. For example, on an overcast day you can compensate for low light by using a fast film (such as ISO 400), enabling you to take pictures without the flash firing. In normal or even bright daylight, an ISO 100 or 200 film is generally fine. Remember that photographs become grainier with faster films.

Glossary

against the light Technique of taking pictures with the main light source in front of the camera; also known as *contre-jour.*

aperture Circular, adjustable opening of the lens that lets light into a camera. Measured in f-stops, the relative aperture is calculated by the ratio of the diameter of the aperture to the focal length of the lens. Opening the lens by one stop doubles the amount of light entering it (see reciprocity).

ASA American Standards Association, which laid down guidelines for mono film speeds in 1943 and colour films in 1944. Forerunner of current ISO film speed rating.

autoexposure Automatic system in which a photosensitive cell measures the light coming into the camera, and sets an appropriate shutter speed and aperture to the film speed and lens in use.

autofocus Electronic system that automatically refocuses the lens for sharp pictures, used on about 90 per cent of modern cameras.

ball and socket Adjustable device used for attaching a camera to a tripod which lets you position it at any angle.

blur Lack of sharpness in picture due to camera shake or too slow a shutter speed.

bracketing A group of exposures taken together one or two stops above and below desired exposure to try to ensure best result. Variation of aperture or shutter can be used.

B setting Long shutter speed mostly used for shooting at night; the shutter remains open as long as the shutter release is kept depressed.

burning in Technique to give more exposure, when printing, to details that have too great a density in the negative (see dodging).

cable release Off-camera shutter release allowing the camera to be fired on a tripod from a distance.

catoptric and catadioptric Optical imaging systems involving the use of mirrors only (catoptric), or lenses and mirrors (catadioptric). Normally used in telephoto lenses.

circle of confusion Diameter of an image of a point of light as it is formed and reproduced by a lens. There is never an ideal point, because of lens imperfection. The larger it is the more blurred a print will be. 1/100in is accepted upper boundary.

composition According to Matisse 'the art of arranging in a decorous manner the various elements at the photographer's disposal'.

contrast The degree of difference between the darkest and lightest parts of an image.

cropping The trimming of a print to improve composition, by covering unwanted areas or by printing only part of a picture.

definition Indicates the fineness of detail in either a negative or positive print. Affected by the ability of the lens and the photographic emulsion to resolve distinct lines, and the scale of contrast of the emulsion.

depth of field The area beyond and before the focusing point of the lens that is acceptably sharp (see circle of confusion). This is dependent on subject distance, focal length, aperture and circle of confusion.

developer, development Converts the invisible (latent) image created during exposure into a visible image. Done by changing the silver salt compounds in the film that have been affected by light into black metallic silver.

diffusion Making an image less sharp – done by placing any light-scattering medium, such as a filter, in the path of a beam of light to soften it.

dodging A printing control method in which dark areas of a print are locally shaded during exposure, to reduce light from the enlarger reaching the printing paper (see burning in).

drying Films must be dried in a dustproof place to eliminate particles of dust affecting results or causing scratches. Prints can be dried naturally and blotted to take away fluff.

emulsion A sensitive coating on photographic plates and films consisting of fine silver bromide grains suspended in gelatin.

enlarger Essentially a camera in reverse, making large prints from small film images instead of small replica images of large scenes. Uses a lens to project the image onto printing paper; illumination is artificial via a bulb through either a condenser or diffusion source.

enprint Commercial small print, from a full negative, usually 9 x 6cm, produced from large output automatic printer.

exposure Amount of light allowed to reach the film when taking a photograph. Reliant on a precise combination of aperture, volume of light let in, shutter speed and film speed.

extension tube Metal ring fitted between the camera and the lens to increase distance between lens and film to allow you to get closer to subjects for greater magnification.

fast lens A lens with a particularly wide maximum aperture stop to let more light into the camera: especially useful in dim light. Some modern fast lenses can operate at f/1.

field of view The maximum angle of a scene a lens can capture.

fill-in Secondary light source common in studio portraiture to lighten shadows caused by main light source.

film Light-sensitive material usually comprising a light-sensitive emulsion coated onto a flexible base. Films for still photography are available in three different types: sheet film for large format cameras, roll film for medium format cameras, and perforated film, the most common of which is 35mm film used in compacts and SLRs.

film speed A measure of a film's sensitivity to light, usually given as an ISO number. The larger the number the more sensitive the film. The most commonly used film speeds are ISO 100 and 200.

filter Transparent sheet of glass or gelatin that modifies the light falling on the subject or passing through the lens. Mainly used to correct the colour sensitivity of the film; also to distort certain colours for greater contrast with black and white film, and, with polarizers, to reduce reflections.

fisheye lens Super-wideangle lens usually giving a 180° field of view. Because of the width of view and massive barrel distortion, the image is distorted into a circle or near circle and depth of field is virtually from the front of the lens to infinity.

fixing Chemical process following the development of films and paper that makes them insensitive to further action of light. The fixing bath removes particles of unexposed silver from the emulsion to prevent more light action.

flare Light scattered within the lens that creates circles of bright light on the surface of the emulsion, reduced but not eliminated by a coating on the lens.

flash Light of great intensity and short duration for cutting out shadows on subjects, bringing out subjects at night, or special effects. Modern flash units have autoexposure control that tells you the amount of flash needed.

focal length The distance from the optical centre of the lens to the point of principle focus. It controls the scale of the image on the film. Wideangle lenses give a small image; telephoto lenses give a larger image. Focal length and image size are proportional – a lens with double the focal length gives double the image size. Generally, the greater the focal length the smaller the field of view.

gelatin Naturally occurring protein used to bind silver halides in photographic emulsion.

grain Granular texture of image that appears in processed photographic materials. Made of minute particles of black metallic silver that form during development. The faster the film, the coarser the grain; grain size is also increased by overexposure or prolonged development of the negative.

guide numbers Used in calculation of correct exposure with a given flash. The guide number given for each film speed divided by shooting distance gives the appropriate aperture. A guide number of 33 from a distance of 3 metres means you use f/11 for a correct exposure.

half-frame Negative size of 18 x 24mm – half that of the normal 35mm negative – which means you get 72 half-frame pictures on a 36-exposure film.

hotshoe Electrical contact on top of camera for fitting electronic flash unit which enables flash to synchronize with shutter.

hyperfocal distance (HPD) When the lens is focused on infinity the HPD is the nearest object to the lens still in focus. When the lens is focused at its HPD everything between infinity and half the HPD will be rendered sharp.

ideal format Name applied to the 6 x 7cm negative size. This is because it fits into the standard sizes of printing paper unlike 35mm and 6 x 6 – and none of the negative is lost, which happens with 35mm and 6 x 6.

incident light metering Use of an exposure meter to measure, from the subject, the intensity of light from the source. So it is the light falling on the subject which is measured rather than reflected light (as is the case with cameras' built-in meters).

infinity Distance from the camera so remote that rays of light coming from objects at 'infinity' focus on the plane of the film in straight parallel lines.

infrared photography Possible with special infrared film that detects energy given off by heat. Used by many photographers for special effects, as green leaves emitting infrared appear black on the neg and white when printed. Can be used with standard 35mm cameras and processed by most developers. Colour IR film is also available.

ISO International Standardization Organization which agrees on the film speed ratings for worldwide use.

latitude Denotes the range of exposure over which acceptable results can be obtained from a film. Latitude in black and white films is usually greater than in colour, but recent technological advances mean films give decent results at even four or more times over- or underexposure.

lens Used in the camera to form an image of a subject or scene. Most common type are compound lenses made up of a variety of convex and concave elements cemented together and precisely spaced, which correct any aberration or distortions of other elements to produce a high quality, sharp image. Lenses come in many forms, including wideangle, telephoto, mirror, fisheye, fixed and variable focus.

light Most important ingredient in photography, as without light pictures are not possible. Photography has been called 'painting with light' – a term that also applies to a method of lighting large, dark interiors. Light sources in photography are natural (daylight, known as available light) or artificial flash or studio lighting set-ups.

macro lens A lens capable of focusing on objects very close to the camera without using supplementary attachments. True macro lenses should reproduce life-size images on the film.

motor drive Device, which may be built in or added to a camera, that automatically fires the shutter and winds on the film after each exposure. Modern cameras offer single or continuous shutter operation and variable speeds.

movement Important factor in photography, which determines shutter speeds and how you photograph certain objects. The ratio between moving objects and shutter speeds is proportional: the faster the object moves, the faster the shutter speed must be to catch it correctly without blur. Has been helped with the introduction of predictive autofocus systems in modern cameras, which calculate where a moving subject will be at any one time and make appropriate adjustments.

multiple exposure Taking several exposures on a single frame of film, usually for special effect. Some cameras have multi-exposure mode to get such a result.

negative Image on photo-sensitive material in which all normal tones are reversed. It enables you to print a positive which will return tones to their normal state.

neutral density A filter used to reduce the brightness of an image without affecting any other variables such as tone.

night photography Special area of photography requiring its own techniques and modes. Without natural daylight you need artificial lights such as lamps or car headlights to make it practical.

O-rings Seal used in underwater and weatherproof cameras to keep out water.

parallax Effect of divergence between the image in the viewfinder and what is actually taken by the lens. This is due to a degree of displacement of the optical axis of the viewfinder and the lens.

PC socket Connection from the camera to a flash gun which triggers the flash to fire just as the shutter is open.

pentaprism A five-sided glass prism in SLRs which allows the image to be seen as it is; without it the viewing screen shows the image upside down and reversed.

printing Process of making an image by exposing sensitized material to light passing through a negative or positive transparency. It is made either with the negative in contact with the sensitized material (contact printing) or by projecting an image of the negative onto the material (projection printing) or, more commonly, by enlarging.

programmed shutter Shutter with a continuous range of exposure settings obtained by interlinking the lens aperture and speed adjustment, for one exposure combination at each exposure level. Usually found on automatic models, programmed shutters do not have optional aperture/speed combinations at a given exposure level.

pushing Uprating the ISO speed of the film and compensating for the underexposure by developing the film for longer than normal. As a rough guide you would extend development by 50 per cent if the film was pushed one stop.

rangefinder Enables a photographer to measure the distance to his or her subject without moving. Rangefinders work by viewing the subject from two viewpoints in the camera 5cm apart. The angle formed between them and the subject indicates the distance. The angle becomes smaller with increased distance and the rangefinder is more accurate with shorter distances (up to 20m).

reciprocity Reciprocity law states that as long as the exposure remains constant (via shutter and aperture combinations) the response of the emulsion is the same. Photographic emulsions do not follow this law when there is very low light with long exposure or very bright light with very short exposure. This wavering is reciprocity failure, which is corrected by increasing the calculated exposure. In colour photography reciprocity failure is more complicated as it also affects colour balance. Appropriate modifications can be made with correction filters.

resolution Ability of a lens or film to produce an image where fine detail can be discerned. A lens with a good resolving power is one which allows the finest detail to be read. Even with high quality lenses, the resolution of lens and film together is improved by stopping down to approximately f/11.

shutter Mechanical, automatic device that opens the lens to let light into the camera for a specific period of time. Shutters mainly fall into two types: diaphragm type is made up of blades attached to an outer ring which pivot to open the shutter; focal plane model features two blinds on rollers close to the film plane.

slave unit Gadget used to provide secondary flash coverage which is activated at the precise moment the first flash fires. Has a photo-electric cell connected to second unit which reacts to the first flash.

slide film The most brilliantly clear film available, slide film can be used in 35mm and medium format models and usually comes in 5 x 5cm size mounts to be viewed by projection. Slide images are purer than prints because they are seen by transmitted light rather than reflected from a paper base.

speed Term applied to light sensitivity of specific films or plates – the faster the speed the greater the sensitivity to light and the shorter required exposure.

spotmeter Type of exposure meter which allows accurate reading of the intensity of light from a very small and distant area.

stop bath This is a solution of acid in water used for washing films and papers after developing and before fixing. It stops the development process dead and prevents any remnants of the developer being carried over to the fixing solution.

stopping down The reduction of the opening of the diaphragm aperture (say from f/8 to f/11), which cuts down on light entering the lens and increases depth of field.

telephoto lens Lens that gives a larger image of subject than a standard lens without the need to move closer to the subject.

test strip In film processing, a narrow strip of sensitized material used to find the most suitable exposure. The strip is exposed to light section by section so each part gets a constant multiple of the exposure given to the preceding one.

tinting Hand-colouring of black and white prints with dyes or paints. Works best on the light areas of a print and can be done for one colour – say, sepia – over a print, or for parts of a photograph tinted in different colours.

uprating See pushing.

ultraviolet (UV) Light that is especially strong on misty days, at high altitude and near the sea. It can affect the photographic emulsion and lose definition, though will not be seen by the human eye. Combatted by UV filters, which are colourless and do not affect the exposure in any way.

wideangle lens Lens that presents a wider angle of vision than a human's. Lenses which give a wider angle of view than 60° are designated wideangle while those over 90° are classified as super wideangle.

zoom lens Lens constructed so its focal length can be altered during operation. The image size of the subject can be increased or decreased at will within the limitations of the lens. The lens range is always shown (for example, 35–105mm).

Index